Praise for Louie Anderson's *Dear Dad*:

"I always knew that Louie Anderson could make people laugh till they cried. What I didn't know was that he could equally move you with his insights, both sweet and bittersweet, about his family and family life."
—Brandon Tartikoff, President, NBC Entertainment

"Engagingly candid . . . He is not after blame but self-understanding and insight into the links between cruelty and comedy."
—*The New York Times Book Review*

"Louie plucks us from the audience and plants us squarely on the stage of his most intimate life. Sometimes laughing, many times crying, the reader is compelled to join the search for Louie's relationship with his alcoholic father."
—Jack Mumey, author of *Loving an Alcoholic* and *The Joy of Being Sober*

"You laugh, you cry, and you learn. It's a wonderful book."
—Suzanne Somers

"A poignant, touching memoir . . . Anderson is an alchemist, transforming misery into the gold of his career."
—*Publishers Weekly*

"*Dear Dad* . . . has the emotional weight and truth of the classic English accounts of discovering elusive fathers. . . . And it's funny."
—*Booklist*

PENGUIN BOOKS

DEAR DAD

Louie Anderson, the comedian and author of *Goodbye Jumbo...Hello Cruel World*, grew up in St. Paul, Minnesota. A frequent guest on "Late Night with David Letterman," "The Tonight Show," and "Arsenio Hall," he has starred in four HBO and Showtime specials.

DEAR DAD

Letters
from
an
Adult
Child

By Louie Anderson

PENGUIN BOOKS

PENGUIN BOOKS
Published by the Penguin Group
Penguin Books USA Inc.,
375 Hudson Street, New York, New York 10014, U.S.A.
Penguin Books Ltd, 27 Wrights Lane, London W8 5TZ, England
Penguin Books Australia Ltd, Ringwood, Victoria, Australia
Penguin Books Canada Ltd, 10 Alcorn Avenue,
Toronto, Ontario, Canada M4V 3B2
Penguin Books (N.Z.) Ltd, 182–190 Wairau Road,
Auckland 10, New Zealand

Penguin Books Ltd, Registered Offices:
Harmondsworth, Middlesex, England

First published in the United States of America by Viking Penguin,
a division of Penguin Books USA Inc., 1989
This edition with a new introduction by the author
published in Penguin Books 1991

LIBRARY OF CONGRESS CATALOGING IN PUBLICATION DATA
Anderson, Louie.
Dear Dad: letters from an adult child/by Louie Anderson.
p. cm.
ISBN 0 14 01.4845 0
1. Anderson, Louie. 2. Adult children of alcoholics—United
States—Biography. 3. Comedians—United States—Biography.
I. Title.
HV5132.A53 1990
362.29′23′092—dc20 90–43252

Printed in the United States of America
Set in Palatino
Designed by Michael Ian Kaye
Illustrations by Robert Zimmerman
Calligraphy by Brian Thomas Merrill

This book is lovingly dedicated to:
Tommy, Lisa, Billy, Shiela, Jim, Shanna,
Roger, Mary, Kent, Rhea,
and Mom

Acknowledgments

I would like to take a moment to thank a number of people. I don't know them all by name. But they're the ones who've come up to me before and after my shows and shared a private bit about their families. Whenever one of you said, "I think I grew up with the same mom or dad," it made me feel less alone, like I had another family out there who understood me. I'm as much your fan as I hope you are mine.

I would also like to thank the many people I worked with in show business who encouraged me to stick it out, and for loving me even when I didn't love myself.

A special thanks goes to Todd Gold, who helped a poor kid from the projects spell words write and gave my letters the structure they needed so you could enjoy them.

Thanks to Jim Gitar and Tracy Kramer, who kept pushing me to be more than I thought I could and loving me despite the mistakes I made.

Thanks, finally, to my mom for never giving up and for going out at five a.m. to get us warm bread from the bakery, to make up for the night before and to make us feel special, and for teaching me the value of a toaster cord.

Contents

Introduction

Dear Friends

Dear Dad was originally a bunch of letters to my dead dad
(that was dark humor; I hope you laughed). Then my ego
somehow got hold of the idea that these letters could be a
book, and some money would be made; and my heart felt
that maybe some other people would get something out of
such a book. So between my heart and my ego, not to
mention my agents, lawyers, accountants, and the great people at Penguin USA, the deal was struck.

After the book was published I went on a twenty-city tour.
This was very hard work, but my ego loved all the attention
and my heart was truly moved by meeting so many people
who seemed to have experienced the kind of life that I had.
It was overwhelming, and made my heart feel less lonely.

I have done a lot of fun things in show business, from the
Arsenio Hall show to taking my mom to the White House,
but there is nothing that comes close to my experience with
Dear Dad. The growth it carried me through, and the love
and letters that I received from the people who read it, have
changed my life. It has also encouraged me to challenge
myself to continue to grow and become the kind of human
being who lives more from his heart and less from his head.

And as for my ego, well . . . How do you like the picture on the cover?

In this new, paperback edition of *Dear Dad* I've included some of the hundreds of wonderful letters I received from you. Thanks to everyone who wrote to me—your honesty and courage made me feel strong, your humor made me laugh, and writing back to you made my hand cramped.

We couldn't use all the letters because we'd have to print another book, but I loved them all. We left off the names, dates, and places to protect your privacy, unless you requested otherwise.

The thing I learned from your letters was that a lot of people in this world are in pain from alcohol and drugs, and that even more people are in pain because they were abused, but the most important thing I learned is that no matter how bad it seems there is almost always some kind of hope. The hope you gave me in your letters will be long-lasting, and I love you.

Love,

Louie

P.S. Many of you have asked me for a copy of the video-tape of my family discussed in the book. I'm afraid it's not of good enough quality to distribute, but thanks for asking.

Onstage, Summerfest - Milwaukee, 1987

My dad never hit us . . . he carried a gun.

Oh, he never shot us . . . he'd just go "Click-click!"

Dads are funny, especially when they're driving. My dad would be driving down the middle of the street with me and my brother Tommy in the back seat. If he saw someone walking down the sidewalk who was a little different, he'd slow that car down, cock his head to the side, lean back, and scowl, "Looook at that, for cryin' out loud . . . get my rifle."

My favorite thing was when my dad would say stuff that made no sense. Like when he was trapped in traffic behind someone who was waiting to turn. "If I was the last person on earth," he'd say, "some moron would turn left in front of me!"

"What?" my dad would say. I'd turn to Tommy, whispering, "I wish he was."

My dad would whirl his head around and snarl, "I heard that. You kids want to walk home from here?"

"We have names, you know?" I'd think. But I'd say, "Yeah, why not. We're a block from home."

"Don't get smart with me," he'd growl.

Just once when he said that I wanted to make the goofiest face and say in my most stupid-sounding voice, "How's this, Dad? Am I acting dumb enough for you?"

If I had actually said that, I would've been the first person on the moon. My dad would threaten us a lot. "I'll drive you twenty-five *miles away and drop you off. That's how far I had to walk to school every day."*

And Tommy would chime in, "And you didn't have any shoes, either. Did ya, Dad?"

"That's right," he'd say. "And when I was a kid, they didn't have any children."

I can only imagine how our kids will explain the hardships of their childhood to their kids. I wonder what excuses they will be able to come up with? Something like, "I didn't get cable until I was twelve. We only had one VCR. There was no spaceship in our driveway."

I think it's harder for kids nowadays. Know why? Because everything is a lot easier. It's so easy it's almost boring. There just isn't much left to do except shave your head and put an earring in your nose.

I understand things a lot better than my dad ever did, but I am also discovering that I've been influenced by him in so many ways.

For instance: When I'm cruising around town and see these kids walking down the street with their shaved heads and their pierced noses, you know what I do? I slow my spaceship down, cock my head to the side, lean back, and scowl, "Looook at that, for cryin' out loud. Get my laser."

Thank you very much, you've been a great audience. Good night.

Dear Dad

It's strange that I said good night to those people. Sometimes, though, you just say things without knowing why. It's four in the afternoon and I am at the Summerfest—Milwaukee, a huge outdoor music-and-comedy festival. It's nice here and people seem like they are having lots of fun. But I don't think I'll ever get used to performing in the afternoon. You can see everybody in the crowd. It lets you know who your audience is. Or at least how they look. Mine seems to be fairly attractive, but, you know, looks are deceiving. I mean, here I am making everyone laugh. People walking by would think, "He's having a great time."

But what I'm thinking and what I'm saying are two different things. Isn't that true a lot? I mean, onstage I was saying, "This is my family. Aren't they funny?" But as I looked out at the audience—women holding babies, men swigging beer, kids being reprimanded by their parents—and as they laughed, I was thinking, "Don't you see, this isn't *really* funny." Or at least it wasn't to me.

Anyway, about halfway through this afternoon's show I asked, "Anybody here with their parents?" I do that in all my shows. A young man, in his twenties, seated in the front, raised his hand and pointed to an older man one seat away. His dad shot him a look that seemed to say, "Hey, don't get me involved in this."

So I started in on his father.

"What's your name?"

"Ed."

"Everyone in the Midwest is named either Ed or Dick," I said. "What do you do, Eddie?"

If looks could kill, my routine would have ended early and he'd be on trial for comic slaughter.

"Mechanic," he said.

"You work on cars?" I asked without wanting an answer. "My dad loved his car. He had a Bonneville. He'd introduce it to people. 'Here's my Bonneville,' he'd say. Then he'd motion behind him and kind of halfheartedly mumble, 'There's my family over there. Thinking about trading them in.'

"No, I'm just kidding," I said. "It's nice that you and your dad are out doing things together. The only things my dad and I did together . . ."

Then—honestly, Dad—I stumbled. I couldn't think of anything to say. I could hear my mind saying, "Make something up, you idiot." I thought for a moment and said, "The only thing my dad and I did together was complain. But I shouldn't complain, because, if my family was normal, I'd probably be asking, 'May I take your order, please.' "

God, I'm glad I got out of that. But really, Dad, what did we do together? I can't think of anything. Or at least I can't think of anything fun. I guess maybe I should complain about that. After all, a boy's got a right to share some quality time with his dad. But it's funny how we're taught not to complain. "Mom," I remember whining on those cold Minnesota mornings, "I hate going to school."

"Don't complain," you'd snap. "When I was a kid, we

didn't have any schools. We had to find smart people and follow them around."

I would mumble under my breath, "I guess you didn't find anyone, did you?"

Frankly, this letter might sound like I'm complaining. I hope not. I've been meaning to write for a long time. Six years ago I got the idea from a friend of mine. I drove him to Duluth, Minnesota, so he could say some things to his father. At first I thought it was kind of strange. Going to a cemetery to read letters to your father? But I cared for my friend. So I dropped him off that bright, sunny day, and when I picked him up two hours later his eyes were red, the letters were gone, and he seemed like a different person.

"Everything okay?" I asked.

"Fine," he said, "just fine." And then he was quiet till we nearly got home. "You know, my dad and I never really got along," he said in a soft voice. "I don't know why. I always hoped we would, but we didn't. It's good, though, that I discussed it with him. I feel better now."

I didn't quite understand, at least then, but I never forgot that day, and always hoped that day would come for me and you. Nine years after your death—today, I mean—it suddenly hit me. It hit me as I was talking to that guy and his dad from onstage and couldn't remember doing anything with you. I remember you and I remember me. But I don't remember us.

I thought about that all the way back to the hotel. I rode in the back of a new Chrysler donated by a local dealer. The guy who drove me was in his late fifties. He wore a blue suit that looked old. He turned around and asked, "Mind if

I smoke?" I shook my head and rolled down my window, staring out at the sea of beer-drinking people in bermudas as he wove his way through the crowd. I don't know anyone in Los Angeles who smokes. But as he lit his cigarette, it reminded me of you and how you loved to smoke. You always smelled of smoke, and there was a yellow nicotine mark between your index and middle fingers that even the undertaker couldn't get out.

"Yeah, smoke and Old Spice," I thought. You always smelled of smoke and Old Spice. You splashed it on after you shaved, but even after a shave your beard was still rough. Someone once asked me what you looked like. It was hard for me to answer, because I never really think about that. Not too many pictures of you exist. But now I can see you as clear as the man who was driving that Chrysler. Only you would have been honking and cussing at the people walking in front of the car. That and you would have had a beer between your legs.

I was glad when the ride was over. I got out of the car, said, "See ya in two hours," and then headed for my room. It's an old hotel where I'm at. The hallways have that musty smell of age, and as I entered my room I wondered if you had ever stayed here when you were on the road with Hoagy Carmichael. All the furniture in my room is new except for a big old desk by the window. It looked like a good place to write something. So I sat down, opened the drawer, found a pad of stationery, and began to write.

Signed,
Trying to remember us

Dear Dad

It's been about a month since my last letter. I may have stopped writing, but I didn't stop thinking about you.

Tonight is very cold, almost like a winter evening, though such a thing doesn't really exist here.

Winter in California always strikes me as funny. I watch snowstorms sweep through the Midwest on the news and laugh. As a matter of fact, I'm in my Jacuzzi right now. "Jacuzzi" is the name of the guy who invented it, a well-known fact out here, where sitting in the warm, bubbling water while the rest of the country is under six feet of snow is normal.

I like to think of my Jacuzzi as a womb, a protective little bubble that I can slip into and disappear from the world. Actually, I never wanted to leave the womb. That was a dark day. I remember the whole thing—at least the way Mom tells it.

It was March 24, 1953, and around five in the afternoon. I remember Mom being very aware of the time, because the Green Stamp redemption place was only open till six. She'd been saving these books of Green Stamps for three years, or at least since the last kid was born. The place was on the way to the hospital and she never could get there unless she was going to the hospital.

So her water breaks at about four-thirty. For me, I guess,

it was like sitting in a nice, warm Jacuzzi and somebody suddenly pulled the plug, letting all the water out. Dad, from what I hear, you were watching TV, probably mad that you had to leave before the five o'clock news for something as trite as the birth of your tenth child. You must've thought it about as exciting as filling up the car with gas.

The way Mom tells it, you went out and warmed up the car and she followed after instructing the rest of the kids to be good and to not fight. You were about to drive off and she said, "Wait, I forgot something." She went inside and returned a moment later, clutching several thick, rumpled books of S&H Green Stamps. All the children had fought over who got to lick the stamps and put them in the book.

"For Christ sakes, what are you doing with them?" you growled. "The hospital doesn't take Green Stamps."

"I know," Mom said, "but the redemption center is right on the way to the hospital, and it's so far downtown, and I never get a chance to go."

"I hope you don't have that kid there, because I'm not delivering it. And I'm not going in there, either. You're going to have to do it. Besides, I don't know what you want."

"Well," Mom started in as you drove. "There's a cute little coffee table, a wonderful blue lamp, not to mention a small umbrella rack that I like. They also have some beautiful mirrors."

"How much time do you think you have?"

"Well, they close at six."

"Oh Christ."

You brought me home from the hospital five days later, my first trip in the back seat of your car. I rode home staring at myself in the mirror Mom had picked up at the S&H center. All the time I grew up, it was in my bedroom. There were always lots of things in my room that didn't seem to belong to anybody. Then I figured out that Mom was a pack rat. I'd ask her who that box of toasters belonged to and she'd say, "You never know when you're going to need them."

"But they're all broken," I'd say.

"Well, your father's going to fix them."

"And then what."

"And then they'll work."

"But, Mom, they're junk."

"Well, the cord's worth a quarter."

I could have been lost in there among the boxes. Sometimes I felt like crawling in those boxes and disappearing among the toasters. I'd always think, "Dad, when are you going to get around to fixing these?" I remember when you fixed the TV. We had to watch *Bonanza* with our heads tilted. "Is Hoss thinner, Dad?" I'd ask.

You could fix anything, Dad. Especially if it worked. "Give me that radio over there," you'd say. "I'll be able to pick up Holland when I'm done with it." While taking the back off, you'd get shocked and your hand would jolt back. "Unplug it!" you'd yell. "What, are you trying to kill me?"

I'd stand to the side and shrug. Maybe.

The other day I got to wondering if that old mirror ever got thrown out with the toasters. I called mom. And guess what? She not only had the mirror, even though she's moved several times; she had all those old toasters. Cords are worth fifty cents now, she told me.

Like always, she started in on what a bargain that mirror was, "just two books," her car was in need of transmission fluid, and as she was about to hit her stride, I interrupted.

"Mom, what about Dad first attracted you to him?"

She was suddenly silent, a rare occurrence. I'd caught her off guard. I'd caught myself off guard, too. In that awkward moment of silence, I thought about bringing up the toasters again. But I didn't. I waited for her answer. After a long pause, she finally answered.

"Well, I was a girl in a small town and he was a musician ·in a band. His life was more exciting. I liked him and, uh, I had a car. And I think he liked me. At least he liked my car. I was the only girl in that town to have my own car. My father got it for me. It was a 1929 Buick."

There was a trace of emotion in her voice that I hadn't heard before. It was like a schoolgirl talking about her long-lost sweetheart, which I guess you are. I've never really thought about Mom as being young and dating and having fun with boys. And it's hard for me to think of you as someone's sweetheart. I guess kids just never think of their parents as lovers. Or as people with lives separate from their children. I wonder how you proposed to Mom?

I wanted to ask Mom, but didn't. She was already off on something else and I had so many questions to ask her about you that I was too confused to follow it up. There was so much about your life I didn't know. I did manage to bring up the mirror. "If you still have it, Mom," I asked, "could you send it to me?" Before I finished my sentence, she started telling me how she could send it.

"Well, I guess I could UPS it," she said. "Or I could overnight it. What is that? Federal Express? But that's so expensive . . ."

Signed,

Mom, I got to go

Dear Dad

It's been a long day. It started with a phone call early this morning. I've never been a morning person. Neither were you. It was Mom who called. She wanted to see if her room was ready. Not here, of course. Not in my house. I have fifty-four stairs up to the front door. She's only visited me once. From then on, she's always stayed in hotels.

We're going to Las Vegas together. Not together, actually—we're going to meet there. Did you ever fly with Mom? From the time the plane takes off till the time it lands, she gives you the history of the world from her perspective. It boils down to salt and pepper shakers and oak furniture and whose kids are on drugs.

One time we went to Europe together. It was a thirteen-hour flight. Twenty minutes into it I turned to her and said, "Mom, you've got to shut up. I love you, but I don't care about Woolworth's anymore." After an hour I had strapped on five seat cushions and was looking for an exit.

Dad, it's so funny how, whenever I start talking about the family, everything turns into a routine. I bet I have one hour of material on you and Mom alone. Being one of eleven children is, for a comedian, like falling into a gold mine. I started developing my routines at the breakfast table, staring at Tommy. "Mom, Louie's looking at me," he'd say in a whiny, baby voice.

I remember doing that to him. God, that used to drive him crazy. My response to Mom was great.

"What? Is it against the law to look at people?"

She'd go back to fixing breakfast and I'd mumble, "Hey, Tommy, what happened to your hair?"

"What?" he would say.

"Your hair, it looks like a girl's hair."

He would march back upstairs and comb it until it looked different. Then he'd rejoin breakfast. I wouldn't look at him at first, and then, all of a sudden, he would look up and I would be staring at him, smiling.

"Whaddya looking at?" he'd say.

"My new little sister, Thomasina."

He would swear under his breath.

"Oh, my dirty-mouthed little sister," I'd snipe.

That's the kind of stuff that can put someone over the edge. It would never get that far if you were at the table, but you were rarely there. You were either sleeping off a drunk or at your early-morning job.

Tommy and I were always the little ones, numbers ten and eleven. We were almost like grandchildren. I was so mad when he was born. I was supposed to be the last kid. The baby. Then he came along. I vowed to destroy him. That's what little brothers are for, isn't it?

Ironically, over the years it's worked out that, of everyone in the family, we're the closest to each other. I call him all the time just to ask, "How's my little sister, Thomasina?"

Anyway, Mom wanted me to have a rundown on the whole family before we meet in Vegas. Funny thing is, she only wants to talk about the ones who are doing well. But the more I think about all of us, it's amazing that we're not all in a mental institution. Of course, some of us Andersons have spent some time behind locked doors or bars of one kind. People don't usually admit they have crazy people in their family, but they're coming from somewhere. There isn't just one couple in Minnesota having them all.

I guess the thing that drove me crazy was your drinking, and nobody in the family really wants to talk about that—except me. I want to talk about it. Let's talk about it, Dad. What do you have to say?

Mom said that you always drank, but that it didn't start affecting you until you got a little older. That's how she remembers it, anyway. I remember that you always drank and that it always affected you. It affected me, anyway. You were already fifty years old when I was born, so, compared to other kids, I had an older father, almost a grandfather.

I can remember coming home from school and knowing when I walked in the door whether or not you had been drinking—without even seeing anyone. That's how sensitive I think I became. I could just tell by instinct when you had been drinking. When you drank at night you'd sit in the room right next to the kitchen, and every time you sipped, the back of your head would tilt back around the corner. We'd see your head bob up and down like a cork floating in a pool.

We would often anticipate how the night would go by how much you would drink. Usually, you'd buy a case of beer and wouldn't go to bed until you drank every last drop. Occasionally, I would work up my nerve and, when you would go into the bathroom, I'd open a couple bottles and pour them out. I guess that was my way of saying, "Please don't drink any more."

We all knew the night was going to get really bad when you downed the last beer and then pulled out a gallon of wine. The stress on us was enormous. Exhausted after one of these evenings, I would fall into bed, only to be woken up a few hours later by a voice loud enough to rattle windows. You'd be calling Mom a whore. Lots of times then, you'd open my door, flick on the light, and yell, "Hey, lard ass, when ya going to lose some weight?"

I don't think you loved me. Maybe you did, but I never felt it. I wonder how the rest of the family felt? No one talks about it, but your drinking did affect us. Roger, Rhea, Jim, Bill, Shanna, they all drank. I did, too, for a while. Like me, they all found a way to quit. But, Dad, your problem became my problem, all our problem.

The really sick part is that somehow I have always blamed myself for your drinking problem. Maybe if he hadn't had so many children, I think. Maybe if I wasn't born at all. Maybe if I had done more to help everyone. Maybe if there hadn't been so much pressure on you to pay so many bills. Maybe then you wouldn't have drank.

Maybe not.

I don't know. I'd like to know, but I don't know how to find out.

Signed,

An impressionable son

Dear Dad

Rhea may have throat cancer. Mom told me the other day. She's in the hospital waiting for the test results. The news frightened me. I mean, Rhea, the oldest girl in the family, is someone who I still think of as my big, strong older sister. She's not supposed to be sick.

Except for you, we haven't had to deal with any other family deaths—thank God. We've been fortunate. There're something like twenty billion people walking this planet, but when you lose a family member, you suddenly begin feeling a loneliness that you can never quite get rid of.

Selfishly, I hope this will finally convince Rhea to quit smoking. Too often people don't think of their health until they're given a stiff jolt of their own mortality. You were that way. You never believed in doctors. Always too stubborn. Mom told me years ago that you had prostate cancer and that you refused to get it treated. I hope Rhea doesn't resist treatment.

I guess it will be your fault if she does, at least indirectly. Parents influence their kids, pass on all their behavior to their children. I look at us and see it as clear as I see you rolling those Bull Durhams in your easy chair. It was a swivel chair, and you'd sit there, tapping out tobacco into a double rolling paper. Sometimes your hands would shake. I would wonder if you knew that. I think you had Parkinson's disease. But you would manage to roll up the cigarette, lick the papers, and then take a deep, satisfying drag.

I tried to roll my own Bull Durham one day. You weren't home. I loved to sit in your chair and act like you. I would pretend to order people around. "Hey, cat, get over there! No slinking around." Then I would investigate all the little remedies for various ailments you kept on the TV tray by the chair. What I remember most were those cough drops, those tiny bitter, licorice-tasting things. They were horrible, but you loved to suck on them. Said they helped your hacking, but I don't think they did. I think it was all in your head, and now all that stuff is in my head.

Anyway, it's all paid off. I've been talking to a network about doing a television show about you. Well, not just you, all of us. But you're the main character, as usual. I've spent the entire day in meetings, discussing the show. I'm calling it *The Johnsons Are Home*. I sat there with the top executives at the network, guys in suits who look like they should be working at banks and brokerages. I explained our family in detail, telling them about Mom and her quirks, all the kids and their problems, and, of course, you. You and your disagreeableness. That was their word. I used something stronger.

I thought I was doing really well. But when I finished, these network guys said they didn't get it. "This family doesn't seem real," one commented. Immediately, I started to rise out of my seat without moving my legs. "What do you mean, not real?" I thought. At that moment, an ally put his arm on my shoulder and gently pushed me back in my seat. "Wait a minute, Louie, let's hear them out," he said. But I didn't hear a word they said. All I could think was,

"Christ, not real. I lived this!" I wished you were there. They'd all be running for their lives.

They said they wanted to soften it a little. I would have liked to. That would have been nice growing up. If you could adjust your family like a television screen, turning the contrast and volume buttons at will. Your contrast and volume buttons were broken. Or stuck, stuck on high. I argued against softening it, and they asked, "Louie, what are you trying to say here?"

The answer was obvious to me. It was about my family. But that didn't seem to satisfy anyone. So I left, saying, "I'll think about it." I wanted to say, "Think about this, buddy," and offer them the same thing you'd give to drivers who'd turn right in front of you without signaling. But I didn't. I got into my car and started out of the studio lot. Before I got to the gate, a guy dressed in costume as some sort of alien from outer space crossed right in front of me.

"Christ, would you look at that," I said out loud.

I sounded like you, but I was thinking, "Hey, that's me." Or at least that's the way I feel sometimes when I think of our family. Like an alien.

In an odd way, that made sense to me and got me thinking about what I wanted from this series. See, I've always had this idea to write a book about a guy who grows up and then has to go back in time and re-grow up and rethink his life. He changes the bad parts and makes them good. He reinforces the good parts and makes them even better. He comes to grips with his family and they come to resolve their problems with him. The story should give people a sense of hopefulness, so that, when they have finished reading, they feel better about themselves.

I guess that's what I want from *The Johnsons Are Home*. I don't exactly want to change everything, but I do want to feel better about myself. And I want to feel better about you. Me and you.

I have this theory that all we deal with in life is loss. We lose the protective comfort of the womb. We lose our mother's breast. We lose the right to mess in our pants. We lose friends, teachers, relatives. We lose our hair, our teeth, and our youth. We keep losing all these things and never get them back, but we never really learn how to deal with the loss. We never really say that it hurts, really hurts, and so we spend the rest of our lives trying to make up for it, holding on tightly to things that we should really let go of.

Signed,

Feeling the loss

Dear Dad

A few hours ago I was at the bank, and a nice woman came up to me and said, "Oh, you're the comedian who doesn't use the F-word."

"I use it all the time," I said. " 'Family.' It's the dirtiest word I know."

She laughed and said, "No, not that one. The other F-word."

"You couldn't mean me," I smiled, "because I use that one all the time, too."

"You do?"

"Sure." I nodded. " 'Father.' It's right up there with 'family.' Almost interchangeable."

She laughed, asked for an autograph, and then left me alone. But it's true, Dad. Words are only dirty depending on your relationship to them. The really bad ones that most people think of were the ones I heard all the time growing up. They came out like an afterthought of your drinking. Put the booze in and the blue language came out until it ceased to have an effect on any of us.

Of course, "family" is a word that was rarely used in the Anderson household. And "father" is a word that had so many different meanings to all of us. To me, "Wait till your father gets home" has always been the single most terrifying sentence anyone could utter. I never knew if you'd be mean or kind, if you'd yell at me or insult me. I only had to hear that and I'd begin thinking about my own favorite F-word. Food.

Not that you're asking, but I think my success in comedy has as much to do with talent as it does with this relentless inner drive I have for wanting to make people love me. In a way, I also want to succeed to compensate for your frustration at having to quit show business. But more than anything, I guess, I really want to be bathed and coddled in the applause of an audience.

It has nothing to do with ego. Things were always chaotic when I was little, and I grew up feeling the uncertainty, shame, and danger of a volatile home life. Because of your drinking, there was a lot of fighting in the house. I never knew if it was my fault or not, but somehow always felt that I played a part in whatever troubled you. As a result, I never felt the security that allows a child to grow up feeling loved.

You fled whatever demons plagued you in cheap alcohol. My escape was food. As you drank and got drunk, I ate and got big. The more frightened I got, the more I ate and the bigger I grew. The more unloved I felt, the more I ate and the bigger I got.

Of course, comedy was my deliverance. I learned to turn the prickly side of life into punchlines. But I haven't been able to turn the punchlines into happiness. I still eat too much, I'm still trying to fill the enormous emotional void inside me by filling myself with food and hoping the warm, soothing comfort of a full belly will last forever. It never does.

Dad, the way I see it, you died without ever confronting your innermost fears, and I'm not going to allow myself to follow the same route. That would be too easy for me. I could sit behind the electric gate of my home and have food delivered every day and never go outside and just eat until I exploded. I could be like you, Dad. But I don't want to be.

I want to change. I want to be happy. And I think the key to understanding my problems is to understand you and your behavior. Your behavior had so much to do with the way I am and the way I don't want to be anymore. I knew you for twenty-seven years and, unfortunately, I really know very little about you as a person. Did you love me? I'd like to know. It's the biggest mystery of my life, and I'm going to try to solve it.

Signed,

Too big to hide

Dear Dad

A package from Mom arrived the day after I spoke to her about you, but I didn't open it for several more days. It was in the shape of the mirror, so I knew what it was.

I finally opened the package last night. The mirror was just as I'd remembered it: colonial-style, framed in mahogany, with a cute little home-sweet-home picture at the top. "I was nearly born in a Green Stamp redemption center for this?" I thought. I can see it: delivered on a table that's worth three hundred books of stamps, wrapped in a towel costing fifteen books, and then dressed in baby clothes totaling fifty books. Imagine the news: "Woman redeems 400 books of S&H Green Stamps, gets bouncing baby boy!"

Anyway, when I finished unwrapping the mirror, I noticed a small envelope had fallen out. I thought, "Knowing Mom, it's the screws." But I picked it up and saw it was addressed to "Miss Toy Prouty." "Prouty," I thought, "that's Mom's maiden name." The envelope was postmarked October 3, 1932, twenty years before I was born. I opened it gingerly, not knowing what to expect, and pulled out two delicate pages of blank sheet music. They were ripped slightly, just starting to yellow, and on them, written in faded pencil, was a letter you wrote to Mom. I began to read.

Darling Toy,

Please excuse this awful paper but I just had to write and tell you how wonderful I think you are and how wonderful you have been to me, and if it were not for you I would have left a long time ago. So you see, I do really care for you an awful lot. And I sure hope I get another one of those wonderful sweet letters from you tomorrow. I surely will be looking for one.

We are on the air tomorrow at midnight, but don't tune in as it will be bad, and anyway I think you should be in bed at that time of night unless you are with me. Don't you think so? Do you? We are on from 12 till one. Well honey, I sure am thankful to have been with you as I am sure lonesome when you are not around.

So please believe me when I say you are just wonderful and everything else that's nice (and I love it). So will bid you a loving farewell until I see you which is soon I hope.

Love and kisses,
Louie

Wow. What a surprise. Love and kisses. I never realized how much a part of show business you were. On the air from twelve to one. For 1932, it sounds exciting. No wonder Mom's always interested when I'm on TV. She misses you being in show business. I think she misses you in general. I can't believe how much about you is revealed in just two pages. A lonely horn player on the road, missing his girl and hoping to see her soon. That's my dad?

Signed,

A lonely horn player

Dear Dad

Kansas City was the first place outside of Minneapolis where I found club work, and here I am tonight, back near the beginning. There are two things I always associate with Kansas City: that both of us worked here early in our careers, and cat food.

Mom once told me that you guys lived here. You were still playing music in a traveling big band, but the few kids you had then were starting to make life on the road increasingly difficult. I guess you were already entertaining the idea of quitting show business, because Mom said you drank a lot. That must've been tough. I can't imagine giving up something as addictive as the applause of an audience.

A few years ago I passed through Kansas City and looked at the house where you lived. It's located in a really poor neighborhood, though back in the Forties it was probably a little better. Mom told me about the place before I left and her description turned out to be perfect. "It was a four-plex," she said. "A dark-red brick building, and it had bars on the windows because it was sort of rough even then, but inside it was comfortable. We had a green sofa and a big kitchen table."

I recognized it before I caught an address. She said that you would come home late after shows. This Mexican guy sold tamales on the corner and the smell would fill the entire neighborhood. You'd be drunk, and you'd stop and buy a couple tamales and eat them by the sidecart, talking with the other drunken men there loud enough so that she could hear you from bed. The funny thing is that Mom told me the vendor was eventually arrested for using cat meat in the tamales, and when you heard about that, you threw up.

The club here is upstairs from a sandwich-and-salad joint, where they happen to serve tamales. Not surprisingly, I've never ordered them. A few of the local comics are also around. It's strange to realize that they think of me as the bigshot in from Los Angeles, the guy who made it. Why's it strange? Because the night I first performed here was the night I almost quit comedy. I don't think I've ever told this to anyone.

It was a cold night, I think, and it was a Wednesday. The opening act was a guy who did prop comedy, and he was okay. There were a few other comedians, no one memorable. Then the guy who booked the acts for the club, a local favorite, went on and did thirty minutes, ending with a real showstopper. He pulled a rabbit out of his butt. That's one magic trick I never wanted to figure out.

It seemed like the show was over. An hour and a half had passed. But then the guy, signaling that he was going to bring me on, gave me the kiss-of-death intro, saying something like "He's a really funny guy, one of the funniest comics in the world . . ." "Christ," I thought, "why didn't he just take a gun and shoot me?" Whenever you tell an audience how great something is, it makes it twice as hard on the performer.

"Hello, ladies and gentlemen," I started. "I can't stay long. I'm in between meals."

No one laughed.

"I guess the last time you saw something as big as me," I tried again, "it was hunting season."

Again, no one laughed. Was it open season on comics? I wasn't too good and I felt really bad about it. I told the guy that maybe he should cancel the remaining two weeks I was booked for and that I should go home. I'd never had this kind of reception. I was used to warm, smiling Minnesota faces, people who seemed to understand my family-style brand of comedy. But the guy assured me that the following night would be better.

For some reason, I believed him, finished out my stay, and was a better person, and comic, for it. Eight years later I'm back again, killing time before two sold-out shows. Earlier, one of the younger comics cornered me in the dressing room and started talking about his career and aspirations. Then he began to drill me. "How many Carson shows have you done?" he asked.

"Nine."

"Nine," he said with the same obvious envy I once had. "Wow."

He questioned me about the different projects I'd worked on lately. I was surprised by how much he knew about me and the other name comics. He was like a sports fan who tracks his favorite baseball players, though, as the conversation slowed, it became obvious that all he actually knew was Louie Anderson the performer, not Louie Anderson the person.

"Do you write your own material?" he asked.

I wanted to snap, "Who else could write this stuff?" Instead, I nodded and said, "Yeah, man, but I lived it first." He shook his head. But I started to think back to when I first started writing comedy, and the truth is that I've never written any of it down on paper. An outline is the most I've ever used. Even the first time I performed I just wrote down key words to signify the joke.

1. freight elevator
2. mommy, daddy
3. breast fed
4. throw rug
5. kindergarten, first, second, third, junior high, high school

I can remember my entire routine:

"I was always fat," I started. "When I was born, I weighed sixty pounds. The doctor had to bring a crane in to slap my ass. When we left the hospital, we took the freight elevator.

"Most kids' first words are 'mommy' and 'daddy.' Mine were 'Seconds, please.' I was breast-fed. Mom went dry.

"Most kids walk to school. My sisters and brothers rolled me there. At nap time everyone had a cute little throw rug to curl up on. I had a braided nine-by-twelve. Do you know what it's like carrying that back and forth to school every day?

"In kindergarten it was 'Louie, no riding the tricycle. Stay off the jungle gym.'

"In first grade I didn't know what a desk was. I wore one for a year. In second grade we learned geography. Guess who played the United States, later to include Canada? In third grade I found the paste—the kind of paste you could eat. Our school had a seventy-thousand-dollar budget for paste, and I was the only kid who didn't go to the bathroom that year.

"In junior high we had swimming. I was harpooned six times. With high school came dating. I had a blind date. She was blind and thought she was with two guys.

"Good night, everyone."

That's how it went. They were good jokes for early material. Over the years I developed them and became known for fat jokes. But early on I knew they weren't as funny as the audience thought they were. At least they weren't to me. Every laugh hurt and reinforced the idea that I was less than others because I was fat. Eventually, though, I even worked that into my act.

"You know, if I didn't do these fat jokes," I'd say, "you would all be whispering, 'Do you think he knows he's that big?' "

Of course I knew. My self-worth was so low that whatever recognition I got from the laughter wasn't enough. I craved more, more, more. Experience told me that people were going to laugh and stare at me anyway, so my joking about it turned into an attempt to control it.

"You know, when I go into someone's home," I'd say, "the first thing I do is head for that wicker."

"Do you eat a lot?" someone once asked me.

"No," I said, "there's a valve in my stomach and every morning I blow it up."

The guy laughed. I cringed.

"Doesn't it bother you to do those fat jokes?" people always ask.

"No," I always say without hesitation. Except these days I'm beginning to feel that I should say yes, because they do bother me. I'm starting to recognize that I've only been denying what I really feel. You know what, Dad? I think if you deny something long enough, you'll come to believe it doesn't exist. Perhaps not physically, but mentally it's true. But I guess what I'm trying to say is this: I've got to stop doing these fat jokes. They aren't funny, and the laughs are beginning to hurt.

If I tried telling something like this to one of these younger comics around the club who see me as a problem-free star, they'd look at me like I was beamed in from outer space. The alien comic who denies his success. All they see are the material rewards. That's all anyone sees. You just never figure the guy who seems to have everything might also have a few troubles.

"Man, your Showtime special was great," one of the local comics said to me a few minutes ago. "You've got it made. I bet you're happy."

"Yeah," I answered.

"Yeah," I thought to myself just before I went onstage. "Happy." I looked in the mirror. "Me? Happy?

"Naaaaah."

Signed,

Always Keep 'em Laughing

34

Dear Dad

Rhea's tests came back negative. What a relief. Apparently, going through everything at the hospital convinced her to quit smoking. That's good news. I hate hospitals. Ever since that visit in eighth grade when you and Mom asked the doctors to try to find out why I was fat. I could've answered them. It was because I liked to eat. I liked to eat in the way that you liked to drink. It made me feel better.

But no, the doctors wouldn't listen to me. Instead, they put me in a room, one of those horrible-smelling hospital rooms scented with too much disinfectant. They asked me to take off my clothes and to put on a hospital gown. Even then they didn't fit me. Then the nurse came in and took blood. I almost passed out. I could never be a junkie.

Half an hour went by, half an hour without anything to snack on, and then, finally, the two doctors came in. A dark-haired woman in her thirties and an older doctor in a lab coat. They were both slim and trim. I immediately felt guilty. They told me my thyroid tests were fine. Fat people always want to blame their thyroid. Not me. I didn't tell where the real blame was hidden. No, I didn't tell them that you woke me up that night at 3:00 A.M.

"Hey, lard ass! When you going to lose some weight?"

When you said that, it made me so mad I wanted to kill you. Instead, as long as I was up, I went into the kitchen and got myself a hunk of cold chicken, a big piece of chocolate cake, a glass of milk, and, of course, an apple to keep the doctors away. Obviously, though, that didn't work.

After an hour of consultation and tests, the doctors prescribed some diet pills and a thousand-calorie-a-day diet. When's the last time anyone stuck to that kind of diet? Anyway, I was nodding to each of their instructions, but thinking, "When I leave this hospital, I'm heading straight for White Castle." Those little burgers couldn't have been more than fifty or sixty calories apiece. I figured I could have fourteen and still have room for dinner.

You didn't go to the hospital that day. Mom took me. You were at work. I can't remember what job it was then. Maybe the railroad. That's what I always said or wrote on the school questionnaire. I remember the railroad job the most, because we used to pick you up every night at midnight. You couldn't drive yourself, because you'd lost your license for drunk driving. God, how you criticized Mom when she drove your Bonneville.

"What? Are you trying to kill us?" you'd snarl. "Christ, get in one lane."

"I've never had an accident," Mom would say.

"Yeah, but you've caused quite a few."

You'd be standing outside the Milwaukee Road Depot, smoking a cigarette and holding your black lunchpail. Tommy and I loved riding in the back seat in our pajamas. I'd always check your lunchbox to see if you'd eaten everything. If you were in a good mood, you'd signal Mom silently and suddenly we'd be pulling into our favorite late-night establishment. White Castle.

The alarm would go off in my head. BURGERS!

"Gut bombs," Tommy and I'd scream.

Mom would already be calculating, "Okay, the burgers are ten cents apiece, fries are twelve. Let's see, why don't we get . . . Wait a minute, I think I have a coupon. Five burgers for a quarter."

"Let me see that," you'd say, grabbing the coupon. "Christ, it's from last year."

"Well, send the kids in with it," Mom would say. "Maybe they'll let them still use it."

They never did, and that was pretty embarrassing. But I still loved those outings. It was like we were a family taking a trip together. Unfortunately, you eventually got your license back, and then the only time we went downtown was to go to the hospital. But we still got to White Castle pretty often, because you spent a fair amount of time in the hospital.

Did I ever tell you that I'm psychic? I made my psychic debut the time you had a bad attack. I got a call from one of my brothers, I can't remember who, after school, and he told me to meet everyone at the hospital. They all had that this-is-serious look on their face. I went in to see you right away. You were on your back and obviously in a lot of pain. Still, you had found something else to complain about.

"Louie," you said, "check to see if they have any doctors here. Or are they all out playing golf? Tell 'em I'm a veteran."

"So is everyone else, Dad. This is a veterans' hospital."

The doctor finally showed up and I joined the others in the waiting room. We milled around that stinky hospital until he finally came out. The doctor looked right at us and called, "Mrs. Gustavson?" We all knew he meant Anderson, but of course, no one said anything. Doctors aren't supposed to make mistakes. Then he left, and returned a moment later with the right name. "Mrs. Anderson?" he said.

Mom approached him and the rest of us followed, not getting too close.

"We really can't say exactly what's wrong with your husband," he said. "Maybe his heart, possibly his stomach."

"It's his appendix," I blurted out for absolutely no reason other than that's what I knew was wrong. "It's burst. You should operate."

The doctor swung his head around and looked down at me, down at this fat, long-haired kid, and he frowned as if to say, "Hey, I'm the professional here."

I kept quiet and thought, "Okay, you'll see."

"We'll run some more tests, Mrs. Anderson," he said to Mom, ignoring me, "and see what turns up."

Five minutes later he came back. If he'd had a tail, it would have been between his legs.

"It's his appendix," he said. "It's burst. "We're going to have to operate."

He glanced at me. I smiled and thought, "Told you so."

I came to visit you several days later. It was afternoon and I remember the sunlight streaming in through the window, cutting a diagonal line across your face. There was the good, light half and the dark, mean half. You were asleep when I came in. I pulled up a chair and sat down. I remember I was eating a candy bar when you finally opened your eyes.

"Looks good," you said in a groggy voice.

I nodded.

"Christ, I'd love a beer right now."

We spoke for a few minutes and then you fell back to

sleep. I sat there, looking at you, my strong dad who seemed at that moment so frail, and thought, "The last thing in the world you need right now is a beer." Of course, the last think I also needed was a candy bar. But both of us clung to our vices like life preservers.

I still wonder why you drank. What fires were you trying to extinguish? Maybe, if I can find out the answer to that, I can understand myself better.

Signed,
There's so much I need to know

Dear Dad

It's too bad you never got the chance to see my house. It's way up in the Hollywood Hills, and every room has a panoramic view of the city as it spreads out seemingly forever. Tonight the cool desert air is blowing and the sky is crystal clear. Nights like these have an almost medicinal effect on the soul.

When I first came to Los Angeles I drove up into the hills and looked out over the city just as I'm doing now. It was then I decided that I would one day live in the hills.

Five years passed before I could afford to get a place up here, but the thought never left my mind. When you have a view as far as you can see, there don't seem to be any limits. Growing up as I did, I thought of nothing but limits. "Be a good child, Louie," Mom always told me. "Don't cause problems. Don't act up. We don't want your father to start drinking."

What a bunch of crap, making me think that my actions caused you to drink.

Your drinking has always been the riddle of my existence. Why, Dad, why'd you drink?

You know, my earliest memory in life is when I was five years old. I was hiding under the kitchen table with Tommy while you were hitting Mom. You were drunk, naturally. You slapped her across the face and called her a whore. Your voice thundered through our tiny duplex like a violent storm.

I remember Jim bolted in the front door and pinned you against the refrigerator.

"Don't ever, ever, do that again!" he yelled right into your droopy face.

The rest of us watched in horror from the other room. I don't know what frightened us more. That you hit Mom. Or that, once you sobered up and realized what had happened, you'd get drunk and angry all over again. Mom had a look on her face that seemed to say, "Oh, what am I going to do now?" As in every crisis, she went to the kitchen sink, turned on the faucet, and washed her hands.

Later, you and Jim sipped coffee at the kitchen table and talked in hushed voices. Mom was in the living room with us, trying to listen in on your conversation as she straightened the doilies on the sofa. She ran her hands over those doilies over and over again, smoothing them as if she were soothing someone's pain. Her pain, your pain, everyone's pain.

I went over to her and put my hand on her arm and began to rub it. I wanted to make her feel better.

"It's okay," she said to me. "Don't worry."

"But why did Daddy hit you?" I asked.

"He was just angry."

"Why?"

"He was upset at himself."

"But why, Mom?"

She didn't ever answer me. Instead, Mom went into the kitchen, started the water running in the kitchen sink, and fixed me something to eat. This seemed to signal an end to the troubles. You got up from the table, parked yourself in front of the TV, and rolled a Bull Durham. Meanwhile, the riddle of my existence continued unexplained.

A few years later, I remember, you and I were out doing errands for Mom. We went by this store and I saw this road racer that cost $4.88. I wanted it badly, like kids get stuck on things. But you said we couldn't afford it. We continued on and then you went into a liquor store and bought a case of beer that cost five dollars. "God," I thought, "that's more important than me? Why was I even born?"

It's always been a mystery to me. We lived at 1122 Hazelwood Avenue, a four-bedroom duplex in the Roosevelt Housing Projects. Mom always boasted that we were one of the first families to move in, but I always wondered what was so great about that. I knew that we were poor. None of the families on TV were like ours. Beaver and Wally Cleaver didn't get their clothes from the welfare store.

I remember the welfare lady's monthly visits to our house. She'd spend about an hour talking to you and Mom, the three of you figuring a budget for the family on this lined paper that had all our names on it. Mom would ask if she wanted something to eat, the signal that it was time to leave. Then you'd walk her to the door and thank her for her help.

"You know, Ora," you'd say to Mom after the door shut, "she's such a helpful woman. We ought to get her a present, a really nice present, like a razor-blade necklace."

When I think about it, I realize that I never questioned that we were poor. We just were and that was it. But there were so many other questions. The Wilsons and their red-headed sons lived in the unit that adjoined ours, and I always wondered why you liked to beat up poor Mr. Wilson.

Most times it started the same way. You'd come home after drinking someplace and stand on the porch, yelling, "Come on out, you chicken-shit bastard!" Mom would be peeking out the window and I'd have a glass to the wall, trying to hear what the Wilsons were saying about you. "Come on out, Wilson," you'd continue, "so I can kick your ass."

"Mom," I'd ask, "why's Dad want to kill Mr. Wilson?"

"Shuush!" you'd say, leaving another riddle unsolved.

By this time, though, everyone was gathered in the living room, huddled together, laughing out of nervousness. Mom ventured to the doorway and tried to persuade you inside. But you wouldn't have any of it. Mr. Wilson had come out and was standing in his doorway.

"Listen, Louie, calm down," he said.

"Don't tell me to calm down, goddamnit," you'd snarl.

"Please don't talk to him, Mr. Wilson," I'd be thinking. "Shut your door. Go back inside. Don't fuel the fire. If you retreat, he'll return to us, and we know how to handle him. We have it down to a science. Please don't let him beat you up again. I can't face your kids anymore, looking at me like it's my fault, like I'm the one who beat you up."

But it was too late. Lisa would turn from the window and give us the latest report. "Oh, he hit him."

With the first blow I'd have the glass up to the wall. "Someone's crying at the Wilsons'," I'd say. "Lisa, what's going on out there?"

"Jim and the boys are trying to break it up," she'd say.

A few minutes would pass, the door would open, and Jim would escort you inside. There'd be blood on your hands. Not your blood. Mom would rush in with a wet, warm cloth to wash off the blood. She'd take care of her baby, calm him down, and the rest of us would disappear.

"Too bad Mr. Wilson can't fight," I'd tell Tommy.

Secretly, I always wished someone would deck you, just once, but the one time I saw you splayed out frightened me in a way your abuse never did. It was a weekend afternoon and you and I were the only ones home. I was watching TV and heard a horrible crash. You were drunk and had fallen down the basement stairs. You were lying there, unconscious. I raced downstairs and tried to get you up. But I couldn't. So I put a pillow under your head and sat there until Mom got home.

"Why is Dad like this?" I asked Mom.

"He's drunk," she said matter-of-factly.

"Why?"

"He's been drinking."

"But why?"

But why, Dad? I'd still really like to know the answer. It's something I think about when I'm sitting on my balcony on a clear night, gazing at the view of the city.

Signed,

Extremely curious

Dear Dad

I remember when people were nice to each other.

That's something I say in my act, and I thought it was appropriate to say right here. It's probably worth repeating, too.

I remember when people were nice to each other.

Signed,

A brief reminder

Dear Dad

Yesterday I finished a week in Las Vegas. Mom was at the hotel with me. I worked every night and she spent the days getting her supply of free hotel articles. Whatever I made for the week, I bet the hotel lost at least half that much on the little soaps, shampoos, shower caps, ashtrays, napkins, and salt and pepper shakers she stashed in her purse.

Mom's so funny. She always tips you off before pulling a heist.

"Louie," she says, "aren't those cute salt and pepper shakers?"

"Hey, Dillinger," I say, "could you wait until we're done eating?"

She tried that at the White House several years ago when I performed there for the Reagans. There was a dinner afterward and we were seated at a large table with numerous foreign dignitaries, politicians, and Secret Service agents. Mom had been eyeing the sterling-silver napkin holders. By the second course that's all she was talking about.

"They're gorgeous, don't you think, Louie?" she said, motioning to me with her eyes that her purse was open beneath the table.

I tried to ignore her.

But by dessert and coffee she was at it again.

"Louie," she said with a wink, "pass me that creamer."

Mom doesn't take cream in her coffee, and unfortunately

for her, it was full and there was no way to discreetly empty it so she could hide it in her handbag. But wouldn't it have been terrible if she'd made me take it and I got caught and tossed in jail?

"Hey, buddy, what are you in for?"

"Creamer."

However, taking Mom to Washington with me was great oneupmanship with my brothers and sisters during Christmas that year.

"What'd you get Mom?"

"Blender. What'd you get her?"

"Oh, I just took her to the White House to meet the president."

I don't know what I'm going to do for Christmas this year. On the plane ride back to Los Angeles, I paged through the gift catalogue that's usually in the seat pocket in front, looking for something special to get Mom. I didn't see anything. Didn't even get an idea.

The trouble is that, coming from a family like ours, nothing ever seems to be enough. What we need, *really* need, can't be bought in stores. I've been slow to learn that lesson. Being poor, you think material goods will provide happiness. But now that I can afford just about anything I desire and still haven't found happiness and contentment, I've learned otherwise.

Sadly, no one in our family ever said, "I love you." Do you realize that? The truth is, I think we were all frightened of saying it, since the obvious reply would've been, "Well, if this is love, what is hate like?"

See, Dad, your drinking caused all of us to build lots of barriers, barriers that no one wanted to risk disturbing because then the safeguards might come crashing down and we'd have to deal with a very harsh reality. So we learned to lie, instead. For instance, if someone asked "How are you?" I'd say "Great." Honestly, though, I'd be thinking, "I feel rotten." You might say that we hide the truth the way Mom hides things in her purse and prays that no one ever checks. It was sure a lot less painful than telling the truth.

I had difficulty sleeping after getting home from the airport. Maybe it was the schedule I'd been keeping in Vegas, maybe it was the anxiety that's been building inside me from not being able to reconcile my relationship with you. I got up, popped a Diet Coke and began sorting through the stack of mail that had accumulated on the kitchen counter. Discarding bills and anything to do with business, I came across an envelope from Mom. The entire week in Vegas, she hadn't mentioned sending anything to me, so I didn't know what to expect.

"Christ," I said out loud, sounding an awful lot like you, "what in the world does she want now."

So much time has passed since that last letter of yours she sent me that I'd forgotten that I'd asked her to send me any other letters you might've written. Who knows what junk Mom has stashed away and forgotten?

Inside was a letter you wrote to Mom from Cherokee, Iowa, in February 1933, only you wrote over the date "still lonesome 1933 times." The rest went like this:

My darling, how are you? Boy am I lonesome for my sweetheart, I sure am. Here it is Thursday and no work. We had two jobs called off on account of cold weather.

Rather tough on me. I had to bum fags here and there and I don't like that. Had I known we weren't working I sure would have been to see my darling Toy by hook or crook.

And say honey you can send me some cigs if you want to. Haven't had any of my own for so long. But don't send a lot, just a few till we start doing some playing once more.

The pencil was smudged on the next two pages and I couldn't make out what you were writing about. But it picked up later.

And I will tell you why she don't desire being married any more later. Well darling, it looks like I won't be able to see you for a while as we have some work the first of every week for a while. But will do the best I can and any way, I might come most any time to stay for a while so don't feel bad.

Well darling, I guess I will say bye-bye and sweet everything till I see you real soon, I hope. My darling, don't forget I still love you and I can love you so far away.

Lovingly, Louie

On the bottom you wrote a string of X's and a big "I love Toy."

Like the first letter, I finished reading and wondered, "Is this my dad?" I never once heard you talk so mushy, let alone utter a single "I love you." I read the letter several more times, paying special attention to the sentence where you alluded to another woman not wanting to be married anymore. "What did this mean?" I thought. Then my mouth dropped open. Oh my God, Dad, were you married before?

Do you know what it's like discovering this whole new person who also happens to be your father?

Needless to say, I wanted to call someone right up and start asking questions. I suddenly needed to know more about you. I needed to know what all my older brothers and sisters knew about you that I didn't. Unfortunately, it was too late to call anyone right then. However, this morning I called Mom and told her that I'd gotten the letter.

"And the article?" she asked.

I forgot to mention that she enclosed a tiny newspaper article headlined "Gleason Likes to Be Paid Upfront." I didn't read it. Mom is always sending me things related to comedy, including the profile the local paper did on her being my mother. "Carson City Mom Becomes Part of Comedian's Stock in Trade" was the headline on that one.

"Yes, the article, too," I said.

But, not wanting to waste time, I came right out and asked, "Mom, was Dad married before he met you?"

Imagine being thirty-five years old and just starting to ask these questions about your father.

"Oh, I really don't want to get into that now," she said, obviously taken aback. "But you know what?" she changed the subject. "I haven't gotten new teeth since 1962 and I could use a new hearing aid as well . . ."

The frustration was overwhelming. Fine, I told her, fine.

I only wanted answers to my questions, and whatever anyone else wanted I was more than happy to pay for. Like I said, Dad, what we need, what I need, *really* need, can't be bought in stores.

Signed,

a big spender

Dear Dad

I just settled into my seat, the last seat in first class, and, lucky me, the one next to it is also empty, so I have the whole aisle to myself. It'll be easy for me to get up and tell the people in coach what a nice buffet we have up here. Even so, I hate flying. The airlines lie to you. When the planes are late, they always blame the weather. When there's a mechanical problem, they never know what's wrong. No way would you let them pull that on you, Dad.

I wish you were with me right now so you could give the plane the once-over. You know, kick the tires, check the engines, check the battery cables, and rough up the pilot. We're sitting on the runway now, delayed, the flight attendant just announced, because of the air traffic. I can just imagine what your response would've been.

"Christ," you would've said, "these pilots drive like your mother. If I took the wheel, this bucket would be up."

"But, Dad," my response would've been, "you don't know how to fly."

"Doesn't matter. I was in the war. I can do anything."

The one good thing about this delay is that the stewardess is breaking out the peanuts early—at least in first class. Peanuts are important on a flight. You don't want to go down on an empty stomach. If the stewardess forgets to serve me, I always clear my throat, hoping to quietly catch her attention and point out the error. If she still fails to notice, I usually raise my hand and politely ask, "Excuse me, but am I in the nonpeanut section?"

Meanwhile, wish me a merry Christmas. I'm on my way from sunny Los Angeles to the deep freeze of Minneapolis, our homeland, to personally oversee and orchestrate my Christmas present to me. This is our first family reunion since the dark day of your funeral in 1979. I've given plane tickets to everyone who needed them, except for Billy, who unpredictably wanders in and out of each of our lives. The only catch was, everyone had to agree to my ulterior motive: to talk about you in front of my video camera.

Strangely, I don't know what to expect from the gathering. I never remember Christmas being much fun for our family. I mean, God, it was never the right tree. There was no money for presents. Worst of all, holidays gave you an excuse to drink as much as you wanted.

We won't have to worry about anyone drinking this year. Everyone who drank—four in all—has quit. But your disease afflicted our family in other ways that I now see clearly by looking at how the lives of my brothers and sisters have developed. Kent has spent some time in prison. Rhea married an abusive husband. Roger was horrible to his wife and kids until he gave up liquor. Shanna, who had an abusive, alcoholic husband, didn't turn her life around till she went through a Twelve Step program. Who knows what happened to Billy? And Jim, Mary, Lisa, Shiela, and Tommy have all struggled, too.

As for me, I can't believe this whole thing is coming off according to plan.

Got to break for dinner and make an announcement to the rest of the plane. I'll let you know what happens.

Signed,

We're getting ready to eat

Dear Dad

It was the afternoon of Christmas Eve when I pulled up in front of Jim's and Jackie's, the place where most everyone's staying, and the sun was shining the way it was the day I thought you had died. I was walking home from school. God, I hated that walk, that long, often cold and lonely walk back to our unpredictable home. I always stayed back and took my time so I wouldn't get picked on.

Also, I was in no hurry to see you, especially if you'd been drinking. So I'd wander the neighborhood, stopping by various people's homes, like an archeologist searching for what was supposed to be normal family life. Mom says that I was as nosy as she was when it came to the neighbors' affairs. "I'd always tell everyone what was happening," she once told a newspaper reporter who was writing a story on me, "and Louie would always ask me, 'How do you know?'"

Anyway, it was a brisk spring day, a real beauty, and I was taking my usual route back home, traveling along the woods, across the railroad tracks, past the street pole that I put my tongue on one winter and didn't cry when I yanked it off, and then down the hill to the creek, being careful all the way not to get my only pair of Huskies, those awful pants for fat kids, dirty. Then I'd cut through to our house. The housing projects, really, but I always referred to it as "our house."

However, one block from home I saw Mrs. Johnson in her yard with her two boys. I said hello, and she replied, "Louie, there was a hearse in front of your house today."

"What?" I said, immediately unnerved and frightened. I wanted to scream, "What the hell did you tell me that for, Mrs. Johnson, you nosy bitch?" Instead, I ignored her phony look of concern and started to run home, hanging on to my books and papers. My mind was turning over the names of all the possible fatalities. You were the likeliest candidate, Dad, but all the while I was praying, "Oh God, please make it Grandma. Make it the person I'm least connected to."

I went in the back door, the quickest way inside, and began scanning the house, taking a mental tally. Mom was in the kitchen, Kent was in the living room. "Where's Dad?" I gasped.

"Upstairs," said Kent, who came over to me in a slow, loving, parental manner.

"It's Grandma," I wanted to cry out. "The one Dad hated, right?"

Kent put his arm around me and said, "Grandma died."

I fell into his arms and thanked God for taking the one person who I could afford to lose, someone with whom I had nothing to resolve, no bad feelings, no anger, and, unfortunately, not much love.

Now picture a room packed full of people intoxicated by nothing more than a party-time spirit, high-volume conversation, and platefuls of sugary snacks. This was exactly the scene inside Jim's and Jackie's place when I finally arrived, the last image I would've used to describe the Anderson family. There must've been fifty people, and everyone seemed to be having a great time. There was lots of hugging, that really tight, warm hugging that indicated everyone was delighted to make contact.

With the TV droning *It's a Wonderful Life* in the background, I stepped by one of my nieces and headed into the kitchen, the place us Andersons love to congregate. There was coffee on the stove, a big coffeemaker full of it, piping hot and strong. Andersons love coffee so much they actually wear out Mr. Coffee makers. Mom was holding court in the center of the room, sitting at the table like a queen on her throne while several nieces tugged at her hands and nephews battled to get her glasses of ice water.

You know, Dad, in her old age Mom is a picture of strength worthy of reverence. She held out. She never gave up. She outlasted you, the toughest man she ever met, and I think she's proud of that. She obviously enjoys the abundance of the Anderson clan, an impressive sight, really. In addition to her eleven children, there are thirty-five grandchildren, and twenty-four great-grandchildren.

I waded through the swamp of kids, said my hellos, and by then it was finally time to sit down at the dinner table. It took all five women and Mom to prepare the meal, which looked more like a medieval feast than any dinner spread that I've ever seen, but we ate just about all of it. We're all big eaters. Andersons love meat, potatoes, corn, salad, butter, sour cream, and bread. Lots of bread. If there's no bread, there's no meal. When I was small, I remember someone always saying, "Are you going out? Well, pick up some milk, some eggs, and some bread." It was five loaves for a buck.

Growing up, meals were our only group activity. They were the only time when we'd all get together and share the bonds of kinship. We loved to eat, no question about it.

It was our salvation from you, something your drunken outbursts couldn't take away from us, and as addictions go, it was perfectly acceptable. So was laughter. During mealtimes, nothing was sacred. The joking began with the first course and continued right through the last bite of dessert. Everyone loved to laugh. You, too. It was a good release, and we loved to see you do something human.

Always, though, there was that awkward moment of silence when the laughter would subside and we'd look in each other's eyes, waiting to see if anyone was going to say anything serious, checking to see if the tears in our eyes were real. But someone would always quickly initiate another joke and ignite another round of laughter, thank God, preserving all of our vulnerable hurts and fears.

By the end of dinner, the little kids were opening their presents, turning the living room into a toy store that was soon knee-deep in wrapping paper. No gifts were exchanged by any of us brothers and sisters. There's too much pain in the process, too much disappointment, and not enough belief in the holiday. Life, I believe, is never about what you get, but always about what you don't get.

Me, I've gotten the effects of your alcoholic behavior. What you didn't give me, I hope to find out tomorrow when I begin taping everyone.

Are those reindeer I hear on the roof? As I write this particular letter, I'm sitting amid the debris of a festive, dare I say fun, Christmas Eve, a rarity in my memory of such occasions. The quiet compared to the tumult of a few hours ago is deliciously comfortable, more so, I guess, since it'll start all over again tomorrow. Yet, even surrounded by all my many brothers and sisters, nieces and nephews, and whomever else around here that I'm related to, I still have the feeling, not unlike the day Mrs. Johnson told me that a hearse was in front of our house, that you, Dad, you're the one I could least afford to lose.

Signed,
Santa's helper

Dear Dad

Not everyone was asleep. Rhea apparently heard me setting up for the taping and came down to see what I was doing. I'd taken over a little corner in the basement, placing a chair and a potted plant in front of my video camera, and I was just about to bite into a chocolate-chip cookie and survey the set when I was startled by her voice. "I'm ready for my close-up, Mr. De Mille," she laughed.

Rhea sat in the chair while I focused and checked the light, and as she chattered away I realized that the life she had survived thus far was worthy of a book or a movie. Her sweetness isn't much of a clue to how tough she is inside. But she ran away from home at fifteen with a truck driver, married and had seven children, became an alcoholic, and eventually wound up in a mental hospital. She's such a gentle soul, though, and when I began telling her what I hoped to collect on tape, her voice turned into the soft purr of a little girl who still refers to you as "Daddy."

I started to film Rhea with her false teeth out, and when she finds out, boy, will she be mad. She eventually caught on, though, and slipped them back in. Watching her do that reminded me of how you always kept your teeth floating in a glass of water. I'd sometimes think of that before I took a drink, and I'd gag. Or else I'd spend what seemed like hours running the drinking glasses under scalding-hot water, ridding them of your teeth germs, before taking a drink. You'd always push them out when the grandkids came over. It made them cry, and you'd give them candy to stop.

Rhea remembered that, when you doled out punishments, you always gave her a choice between a spanking and not going to the movies for two weeks. She always chose not attending the movies, because she knew you wouldn't enforce the rules. That was typical. In a family like ours, punishment was rarely or consistently handed out. Rather, it was always for something you didn't do instead of something for which you deserved to be punished. This has always played havoc with my mind. If everything's going along too smoothly, I seem to wait for you to barge in my room at 3:00 A.M. and wake me up.

I asked Rhea about her childhood and, like me, she seemed to remember very little. She said that I was always her favorite little kid. "Mom used to get mad at me," she said, "because I would come home late and go in your room and pinch you so I could play with you."

"Thanks a lot," I said.

"I used to dress you up like a little girl."

"Great!" But then I got serious and asked, "Did Dad ever hit me?"

"No, not that I can remember," she said.

To me, it was obvious that your drinking affected Rhea's adult life, but no matter how many times I tried bringing that up, she denied it. She refused to see the connection. But when I asked her if she could say one thing to you right then what that would be, her answer was so obvious that even she couldn't deny it.

"I'd say," she began and then paused to think. ". . . I'd say I wish I would have been a better daughter."

See, just like me, she blamed herself for your behavior. I wanted to say, "Rhea, I wish that he would've been a better father. Don't you?" But that would've been overstepping the understood boundaries that we don't dare cross, and not really appropriate to the situation. It's not my place, I realize, to alter everyone's memories of you. It's not my place to criticize. And most of all, it's not up to me to change everyone in the family.

Mine is a private journey, a selfish one that is full of much more pain than I realized at the start. When I set out several months ago to discover what internal battles caused you to drink, I didn't understand that I'd also have to take an equally hard look at myself. It hurts, Dad, it hurts a lot. But I'm in too deep to turn back.

Signed,

Mr. DeMille

Dear Dad

You remember that time we went into the woods, and not by choice? I should've bolted upright and told you a big "Fuck you!" I was only twelve years old. Mom didn't want you going out. She knew you would drink as soon as you were free from her watchful eyes. To get around her, though, you took me and Tommy along. Used us, didn't you? Said, "It's okay, Ora, I've got some errands to do and I'll take the boys with me."

I didn't want to go on this particular outing. Just as I could tell if you'd been drinking before I walked in the door from school, I could sense the real reason you wanted us to tag along, and it wasn't because you wanted a father-son outing. First you gassed up the car at Joe's. Joe's, I remember, always had bulk oil for ten cents a quart. That was so appealing—anything for a dime. It sounded like such a good deal. I could never figure out how he made any money on a quart of oil, but I bet he made plenty on the gas.

After filling up, everything seemed great, and I was thinking, "Well, maybe we can have fun."

"Hey," you said, "you guys want to get some pop?"

"Where?" I asked.

"Next door."

There was a bar next to Joe's.

"It's starting to snow," I said. "Shouldn't we do our errands and get back home?"

"Ah, come on," you urged. "It's only for a minute."

"But, Dad . . . ?" I whined.

"You fucking baby, come on."

What choice did I have? What twelve-year-old boy wants to be called a fucking baby by his father? Though I was upset, the three of us went inside and sat atop the high stools along the bar. I ordered a Pepsi and Tommy had an Orange Crush, and there we sat, nursing our sodas for three long, tedious, horrible hours. Tommy and I watched in silence as you tossed back beer after beer, getting drunker and drunker and ruder and ruder, hating every second of this nightmarish drinking bout.

It was dark when the bartender finally kicked us out. Actually, he tossed you out and we had to follow.

Meanwhile, the weather had gotten more severe. By the time we got outside, it was snowing heavily, one of those still, stormy nights that are beautiful and frightening at the same time. The white so pure, the sky so gray and ominous. You were really drunk, totally pissed and bleary-eyed. I had a weird experience then, a realization where I was suddenly able to view everything that was happening from afar. It was the first time I can remember seeming to be outside of my body. I saw these three pathetic figures standing alone out in front of the bar in the snow, one of them obliterated, the other two terribly frightened. The scene seemed a foreshadowing of a disaster.

The next moment we were in the car. We were the only ones on the road, our Bonneville making the first tracks in the virgin snow. You drove very slow. We traveled down Avenue B, then made a left onto Ames Avenue, cruising by my grade school. I was thinking, "Maybe you could stop

and let me out. I could go inside and wait there until tomorrow morning." I've always liked the idea of being inside
a school all alone, no one there to pick on me.

However, we continued driving down the winding road,
our speed holding steady, me steering from the side, and
you hacking out that disgusting smoker's cough, sounding
as if broken bottles were being raked inside your throat, and
laughing at the situation as if it was some kind of joke that
we were in such a frightening circumstance. Two turns before we reached home, you started to nod out.

"Let me drive, Dad," I said.

"Shut up, Louie," you snapped.

"But you're falling asleep."

"I can drive," you insisted.

What the hell were you thinking? We made the turn on
Jessimere okay, but there was just one more turn before we
were home. Suddenly, though, the car stopped. It wasn't
the engine. No, you were out cold. What an ugly picture.
The three of us huddled in the front seat—Tommy on the
door, me in the middle, and you in the driver's seat, letting
out loud, raspy snores. Outside, the snow was falling without letup.

Home wasn't that far, but I was too frightened to get out
and run for help. Why? I wanted to protect you, Dad. One
of the neighbors might've found out that you were a drunk,
that you could've cared less about your kids, that you were
willing to risk our lives so you could get some booze. See,
none of us knew who was aware of your problem; we were
shamed by it.

Somehow, though, I mustered up my courage—a moment
of sheer desperation, I'm sure—woke you up, and told you

in the gentlest of ways to put the car in gear and step on the brake so I could slowly guide the car home. But because you were so drunk, you stepped on the gas instead. The car took off, heading at a swift pace for the place we all referred to as "the woods."

The landscape was a stark, seamless blanket of white, and everything went flying by so fast. Your heavy foot slipped and the car was floored. We went careening along the roadside, churning up snow and mud, the Bonneville doors being pounded by tree after tree. It sounded as if we were being shot at. However, despite the speed, I noticed the smallest of details whizzing by. I saw the numbers outside apartments, people eating dinner, my dead grandmother sitting in a rocking chair with perfect clarity. It's what I imagine dying is like. You are on your way out, but not before you see certain things.

In a matter of seconds we flew right over the hill, leaping above the embankment, airborne. I expected a crash, a fiery crash, and then certain death. Instead, we landed in the deep snowdrift with an unexpected poof. It was silent. The snow came up like powder and covered the car. I checked to see if you were all right, Dad. There were no injuries. Tommy was unhurt, too. I told him to stay with you in the car while I got out and hiked to our house for help. I could see it in the distance. The light was on, and I could make out the shadows of people in the living room.

Heading toward home, I reached the bottom of the big, icy hill where we always slid on cardboard boxes or our metal discs. I started to climb, but the first two times I came sliding back down, not quite able to reach the top. On my third attempt, I slid down again. But that time it was kind of fun, and for a moment I forgot all about you and Tommy being stuck in the car. When I finally reached the top, a neighbor pulled up in his car, rolled down the window, and asked if I needed any help.

"Nope," I said. "Everything is great. I'm just going home."

Fortunately, when I arrived at home, some of my older brothers were there. I told them what happened, and they went off and rescued you and Tommy from becoming ice cubes in the deep freeze. Not surprisingly, you hardly woke up as they carried you to bed, and you slept until late the next day. You never apologized, either. You handled it by making fun of the incident, laughing at what could've been my early death. Well, Dad, screw you!

Signed,

A backseat driver

Dear Dad

Mary, the second-oldest girl, shifted in the chair and stroked her arms. She has the sweetest face and a big, hearty laugh to match her red hair. She was never around much when I was growing up, but she started right in with a story about taking me with her downtown on the bus.

"Was I wearing a dress?" I asked, remembering Rhea's comment.

Mary laughed.

"I used to take you with me and pretend that you were my baby."

I don't know Mary very well, but I feel close to her. She used to work at a drive-in restaurant called Porky's, a place whose name always caused me to wince whenever it was mentioned, since I always thought it referred to me. Its logo was a big smiling pig. Mary used to bring leftover food home after work, and I'd wait up for her, and for those few moments she was the most important person in the world.

"Were Mom and Dad the perfect couple?" I asked.

"No! Oh God, no," she shrieked with a big, booming laugh. "No, they weren't. But I honestly think they loved each other. What is a perfect couple anyway?"

Mary's one to ask. The guy she married wasn't exactly Mr. Charm, but Kent put an end to that. He went down there one day and said that, if Mary was beat up ever again, the guy would regret ever being born. Or something like that. But the message was clear.

"What was it like when Dad played his trumpet?" I asked.

This caused Mary to pause and smile, and I could see she was remembering something pleasant, very pleasant.

"It was like he was another person," she said. "Not the same man he was after the rest of the kids were born. He'd close his eyes and play and his body would sway with the music. It was as if he was in another world, a very pretty and peaceful world where nothing bothered him the way it did around the house."

God, what I would have given to hear and see you play. I never did, you know. I've never even seen a photo of you playing the horn. I remember a few times when there was a trumpet resting beside the platform rocker in the living room. But you didn't play it. I wonder, though, if when you performed it was the same as when I'm onstage? You're up there in front of the crowd and every moment is very real. Your heart seems connected to a light, and the truer you are to your heart, the brighter the light gets and the stronger your heart feels, and your eyes see the world spinning at its absolute clearest.

"If you had one thing to say to Dad, what would it be?"

Mary looked up and folded her arms, closed her eyes, and seemed to disappear into a private rapture that was foreign to me.

"If I could say one thing to Dad, right this instant," she said, opening her eyes and looking directly into the camera as if you were inside the lens, "I'd say, 'Play me a song.' "

It must have been a huge letdown to go from recording "Stardust" with the great Hoagy Carmichael to switching trains at night from one track to another and not even being able to drive yourself to and from work because you'd lost your license, and being reminded of this every time Mom pulled the Bonneville into the depot parking lot with Tommy and me waving from the back seat. Maybe that's one reason you drank. You simply hated work. No matter what, though, you always worked, and sometimes you worked more than one job.

Want to know what I thought was your worst job? Grave digger. I never wanted any of my friends to know that's what you did. I had this frightening image of your dark silhouette digging a deep hole while the wolfman lurked behind you. At the time I didn't have any idea about death. I hadn't been exposed to death, except for Grandma, and she didn't have a funeral. The only deaths I knew about were violent ones. A friend's brother was shot to death, and, of course, there was Jennifer White's. God, I'll never forget that.

Jennifer had been dating this guy who went crazy on her one night and killed her. A bunch of us from school went to the wake, and her mother decided to have an open casket, hoping it might save someone else from a similar fate, though I bet her boyfriend never had much luck asking girls out again. Anyway, the sight of her lying in the casket is a picture that'll be etched in my brain forever. She didn't look anything like herself. Her face was all sucked in, and you could still see the wounds from where she had been bludgeoned. It was disgusting, exactly the hideous impression of death I'd expected.

When you came home from the cemetery that day, your head was hung low and there was a six-pack under your arm. But the beer didn't seem as important to you as usual. You were sad and remote, and you slumped down in your chair. Someone asked what was wrong, and you said that you'd just quit. "I couldn't take it any longer," you said.

I learned that you later confessed to Mom that for some reason you had seen a tiny casket that day, not Jennifer White's, but a smaller one. You looked inside and saw a tiny baby girl, a perfectly formed little girl, who had been born dead. You started to cry, and decided right then that you had to quit. I don't remember who told me about that, but I do recall quite vividly realizing for perhaps the first time that this man who I knew only as a mean-spirited, temperamental drunk had within him the capacity to be warm and sensitive. It was a glimpse of character that I never let go of, no matter how hard you tried to prove otherwise.

Before inviting Roger into the hot seat, I reiterated my impression of this spooky job, which made him laugh. "I probably knew him better than anyone," he told me. "See, I worked with him on the rubbish truck."

I didn't know that, though it's not surprising, since Roger was on his own by the time I was growing up. He's the funniest one in the family, no question about it. Roger's also the one who most resembles you. He has your coloring, his voice is raspy from smoking and yelling, and he criticizes everything he disagrees with. He used to drink a lot, too, but he quit a few years back when he saw how badly he was treating his family.

"So what was Dad like when you guys worked together?"

"He was goodhearted," Roger said in a serious tone of voice that sounded eerily like yours. "I remember Dad would see some kid walking down the street who didn't have nothing, and he'd always stop and give him a buck. Always a buck in them days. You could go down to the Salvation Army and get some clothes for a buck. A lot of you guys never saw that side of Dad."

"Why's that, do you think?"

"I don't really know. Dad wasn't the kind of guy who sat down and opened up. He kept everything inside. Maybe he was just tired by the time you guys came along. I don't know. It's a good question, though. Let me know if you find out."

With that, Roger put on the funny mask he'd been prior to the taping, lit a cigarette, and asked if I was going to breakfast. It was dinnertime. What a card. But I guess it takes one to know one.

Signed,
The ace of hearts

Dear Dad

In our house breakfast wasn't just a meal, it was an event. The proportion and significance of it shouldn't be underestimated, especially when it comes to me. Consequently, I've taken what used to be my regular morning menu, thanks to Mom's culinary expertise and stamina, and compiled what I fondly call "Recipe for an Insecure Child." It's nothing I'd like to pass on, but it goes something like this:

Recipe for an Insecure Child

First eat a quick five pieces of toast, heavily buttered. Then hit the hot oatmeal, doused thoroughly with sugar, grapenuts, and milk. This should be slurped down between bites of toast.

After the oatmeal has completely coated the stomach, quickly snatch another pile of toast and begin stabbing the gooey middle of the over-easy eggs. Then munch on a few strips of bacon, some more eggs, which by now should be all mashed up and piled on the toast.

Pause to drink a glass of milk.

Follow this up with the sausage that's been lying in the syrup covering the pancakes. Burp. Then dig into the pancakes.

When those have disappeared, wash everything down

with another glass of milk, then get up from the table and grab your school books and hurry out the door.

Oops, I nearly forgot the last step. Before the screen door slams, lean inside and ask Mom, "Hey, what's for lunch?"

Signed,

As famished as you were thirsty

Dear Dad

After dinner I taped Lisa, Jim, Shiela, Kent, and Shanna in quick succession. With so little time to capture such a large group, things were nonetheless going pretty well. I was surprised that everyone's comments, whether or not they realized it, echoed many of my own feelings toward you.

Generally, everyone said that their fondest memory of you was when you quit drinking late in your life. Their worst memory was when you died. Saddest of all, though, is that everyone also blamed themselves in some way for your alcoholism. That you managed to pull off that trick boggles the mind.

Of course, the two people who I'd most like to tape are you and Billy. Neither of you are here. We know where you are, at least, but Billy, the best-looking kid in the family, could be anywhere.

I'll never forget the telephone call we got several years ago regarding the most mysterious of us Andersons. I can't tell you where it was from, but Mom answered, and from the initial part of the conversation, it seemed obvious that Billy owed someone a sizable sum of money. Listening in, I gathered that he had vanished suddenly and was nowhere to be found. Big surprise.

After a while Mom cupped her hand over the receiver

and, while trying to stifle a nervous laugh, whispered, "He told this guy at a hotel that he was related to the Kennedys, and that he lost his wallet and someone from 'the family' would pay the bill."

It always amuses me to think about this incident, but more than that, I'm impressed by how sharp-crazy Billy is. Can you believe buying a story like that? He must've done some slick talking. I wonder how much the tab was? I bet the guy who let Billy check in under the Kennedy name was sweating bullets over whether or not that tab was ever going to be paid. Imagine believing Billy was a Kennedy!

I wonder how he came up with the idea that he was a Kennedy, anyway. Someone probably said, "Hey, you look like a Kennedy," and from then on he thought it was true. He also probably thought it was a hell of a lot better being a Kennedy than an Anderson. When we were kids, I think all of us fantasized about being someone else and coming from another family. I thought the Cleavers were pretty neat, except June probably wasn't a good cook. Wally and the Beav were always so skinny.

At some point, I guess, Billy quit fantasizing about it and simply believed he *was* someone else. He often spoke of being picked up by beings from another planet. That never struck me as too farfetched a notion. I've thought that about myself on a number of occasions.

Right now, in fact, I'm wondering how I landed in this bunch. The pickled finger of fate, I guess. I wish the commander of my spaceship would beam me back to Los Angeles so I could get on with my life. It's a bit after midnight. A few people are still up, watching television and swapping stories. But with my videotapes packed snugly away, my sentiments toward Christmas are suddenly a lot like yours used to be.

Every December 25, I remember, you'd wait up for the stroke of midnight, yawn like a bored grizzly bear, and then growl an abrupt end to the holiday. "It's twelve-oh-one," you'd say, taking an exaggerated look at your watch. "Now throw that goddamn tree out so I can put my chair back there."

Let me tell you what just happened. I was intending this letter to be brief. I was going to sign off right after that chair line with a melancholy "Ho, ho, ho." But then there was a knock on the door and Kent came in. The oldest of the children, he knew you better than the rest of us. On the tape, he spoke a lot about your talent. He even called you "a great success, considering . . . ," though he was equally hard on you for your drinking. "A real son of a bitch," he said.

"So how do you think it's going?" Kent said. "Is the tape good enough for *60 Minutes?*"

"It's hard to tell right now," I said. "I've got to see it all again in one piece and then I'll know. But I'm feeling pretty good about it. It's just great to get everyone on tape."

"Yeah, it'll be nice to watch it in about twenty-five years," he said, "when we're all too old to hear what we're saying."

Kent was just kidding. It turned out that he'd come in for a reason.

"You're saving Mom for later, I guess, right?" he said.

I nodded.

"And yourself, Louie? Are you going to tape yourself?"

"No, I don't think so. I already know what I remember, and it's not much."

"Well, then," Kent said in that big-brother tone of his, "let me ask you a question. What do you regret most about Dad?"

"I don't know," I said. "It's too big a question for me right now."

Then I thought about it for a moment.

"Maybe that I never heard him play his music," I said. "Yeah, that's it. I knew him as a drunken tyrant, and everyone who did hear him play told me that's when he was his happiest and best. I never knew that side of him."

"I have some music of Dad's," Kent said.

"What?" I screamed.

He pulled two cassette tapes from his shirt pocket and explained that he'd come across a record collector who had two albums with you playing on them. The guy wouldn't sell, but he allowed Kent to tape them.

"Want to hear 'em?" He smiled.

We played the tapes a couple times each, and then, suddenly, I started to cry. The emotional response was overwhelming. I missed you. I missed the man I knew, but more than that, I missed the man I never got to meet.

"You know, everyone I played the tapes for cried," he said. "Even me."

"Christ, he was good," I said to Kent as I wiped the tears. "I wish I'd have been able to know him better."

"I wish I'd gotten to know my dad better, too," Kent nodded, "because, when I did know him, he already wasn't himself. But the thing is, I never blamed him."

"Why's that?"

"I suppose because trying to place the blame on someone always seemed like an impossible task. Like trying to find the start of something that's actually an endless cycle. I just figured it was better to be hard on myself and to make sure that I was a better person to those I loved. That way I could break the cycle."

Did you hear that, Dad? That's the kind of wisdom older brothers are put on earth to dispense.

Signed,

Tired of cycling

Dear Dad

Let me start by telling you the bad news. We've got a new president. The inauguration was yesterday. I was asked to perform at one of the inaugural parties in Washington, but I told them that, unless some mention was made about the homeless situation in this country, I wouldn't do it. Obviously, the show went on without me.

I'm reserving my judgment about the Bush administration, but I am already certain of one difference from the Ronald Reagan years. They're eating again in the White House.

However, it never really mattered to you who was in office. You called all politicians the same thing: stooges. I used to love it when you'd rant and rave about politicians. "They're all a bunch of crooks," you'd say, pointing to whoever was on TV. "Look at his eyes. He looks just like the guy who sold me that junk car out there."

A good tirade could last half an hour. It was great to hear you go on like that. The pressure was off us and on them. The best time was when Nixon was in office, because you loved to blame him for everything. "Goddamnit," you'd bellow, "I haven't been able to find a tool around here since Nixon was elected."

The only guy you ever seemed to like was Eisenhower. I think it was because he once wrote you a letter, a response to one of the many letters you wrote him. But you always denied that. "I like him because he was a veteran," you maintained. "You can trust a man who's been to war."

Ah yes, we don't want to forget you, too, were a veteran, a disabled Veteran of Foreign Wars, no less. But how could we forget? You reminded us of it every chance you'd get. You were always quick to show off your scar. Anytime the subject was raised, your pants were lowered. "See," you'd say, "I was shot in the back."

We'd look and fake a gasp to pacify you, but I always wanted to say, "It looks more like your ass than your back, Dad. Is that because you were running away?" I mean, if you have to pull your boxers down to show your scar . . .

It always seemed that discussion of your war wounds led to a verbal harangue of the president, followed by a letter. "Louie," you'd snap, "get me my cards." You always wrote on your Prizeword Pete contest postcards. For as long as I can remember, you entered that silly newspaper contest. You'd get your Webster's out, look up the different meanings of the words to that half-finished puzzle, then clip the thing from the paper with the scissors only you were allowed to touch. You'd stare at the finished product, checking your work, making sure the glue would hold, and then you'd affix a ten-cent stamp and mail the card off. The grand prize was twenty-five hundred dollars. Cash. You just knew if you won life would be different.

However, you never won. Never even got an honorable mention. But you never stopped hoping, either. I really admired that. You also never wasted those Prizeword Pete postcards. After fetching them, I'd stare over your shoulder as you started a letter and worked yourself into an angry lather.

"I'm a veteran of World Wars One and Two," you'd always start out. "I'm a father of eleven children and a former musician with Hoagy Carmichael."

"This is good," I'd think. "Use all the impressive stuff up front."

Then you'd really get into the meat and potatoes of the letter, complaining about how you'd been treated by the welfare lady, about how you couldn't afford this or that, and about how the country wasn't what it was cracked up to be. And you'd always end it by stating that you were a wounded and disabled veteran.

"You tell 'em, Dad," I'd think.

These letters were always addressed to the same place. The White House. You wanted to go straight to the top dog. It seemed like you felt better after lashing out at the president, telling him off, challenging him to a fight, or something like that, and you would instruct me to mail it on my way out the door. I'd start off, but before I got outside, Mom would pull me aside and read over the card. If it met with her approval, she would let me go ahead. If not, she took it from me and went into the kitchen, where I suppose she tossed it out.

Your maddest letter, I think, was when the government cut you off from your veteran's pay. We didn't have any savings. You weren't going to stand for it. "Louie!" you called. "Get me my paper and pen!"

I was back in an instant, and you started right in. "Dear Mr. President," you started, growing angrier with each sentence and finally working up to where you actually threatened to "personally kick his ass." This time you didn't seem to be blowing steam; you seemed to be downright disturbed.

You didn't ask me to mail it, and Mom seemed too afraid to say anything. She just watched as you stormed out the door, a Veteran of Foreign Wars exercising the freedom for which he fought and was wounded.

When you returned from the mailbox, you seemed to have calmed down.

"I think I'm gonna have a beer," you harrumphed.

No one argued.

The reason I got on to this subject, I guess, has to do with the good-news part of this letter. Mom is coming out to Los Angeles next week so I can tape her. But get this: In preparation for her role, she called my business manager. "Louie said I could get new teeth and a hearing aid," she told him. "I haven't had new teeth since 1962. The porcelain is fine, very good quality, but the liners finally wore out and I think it'd be best if I replaced them."

My business manager said fine, whatever she wanted. But what Mom really wanted was to talk.

"And as for the hearing aid," she continued, "I've checked out two models. One costs seven hundred dollars and the other is fourteen hundred. I don't think my hearing is that bad, so I'm going to get the one for seven hundred. I'll take it on a thirty-day plan, and then talk to everyone I know. If it works out, great; if not, I'll take it back and get the more expensive model. What do you think?"

I'm thinking about changing my phone number.

Signed,

Earth to Mom, can you hear me?

Dear Dad

I put Mom up at the Hilton Hotel in Beverly Hills. Before checking in, though, she handed me half a dozen letters you'd written her during your courtship. I canceled my next appointment and went right home to read through them. They were just like the others.

Dearest darling Toy [one began], I received your wonderful letters and oh what a thrill. I surely hope you mean all you say, and if you don't, I sure will be awfully sad and blue as you are my everything. In fact you are all I have and that's the truth sweetheart, honest . . .

My darling Toy, [went another letter], Am about to go to bed so will say good nite sweetheart and hope we both have wonderful dreams of each other. Wrote you a card and letter, but I just love to write to such a marvelous, wonderful girl as you, and anyway, I love you and guess I can write as often as I please.

Oh God, were you ever a sentimental sap! Each one was more gooey and saccharine than the last. While the rest of the country was in the throes of the Great Depression, you were in love, ridiculously, hopelessly, obliviously in love with Mom. I read these letters with disbelief, over and over again, wondering, as always, why it was that none of us ever knew this side of you and feeling, as you wrote, "sad and blue" and disappointed that we didn't. I hoped that my interview with Mom would fill the void a bit.

While getting Mom ready to sit before the camera, I tried guessing what stories she'd tell me. The one when a horde of cats surrounded her in a barrel or the one about how her wonderful father treated her like a princess or perhaps her infamous confrontation with the notorious gangster Al Capone, a tale I knew about but had never heard.

"Do you think I need more makeup?" she asked me. "How does my hair look?"

"You look great, Mom," I said as always.

"Louie, do I look old?"

I shook my head and finally got her seated in front of the camera.

"Let's start, okay?" I said.

"Should we?" she asked.

No matter what anyone thinks, filmmaking is not easy.

"Now, when I ask you a question, I want you to use that question in the answer," I instructed.

Mom shook her head.

"I understand."

"Like if I ask when you were born . . ."

"In 1912," she interrupted, "in Mitchell, South Dakota."

"Right, Mom, but what I want you to say is, 'I was born . . .' "

"In Sioux Falls, South Dakota," she interrupted again. "In 1912."

"Mom, hold on a second."

I began thinking that maybe I should've hired a stranger to do this. A professional. It's hard to work with your family. It's hard to live with your family, for that matter. I always say, "Family: you can't live with them, and you should kill them." It's a joke. However, after a ten-minute break, Mom and I started again.

"I was born in Mitchell, South Dakota, in 1912," she said in a clear, strong voice. "I was raised by very loving parents. My father owned filling stations. I ran the candy-and-cigarette stands in them. I had one sister, Iona, and a brother, Perry."

Then Mom leaned forward and whispered, "Should I mention my sister Viola, who died when she was born?"

"No."

"You know, Louie," she continued, "you were named after Perry. Your middle name. My father was a generous man. He always tried to help people out. In fact, he helped them out too much and was cheated out of the stations by a crooked lawyer."

It was difficult for me to keep my train of thought after Mom mentioned that she was raised by loving parents. Loving parents. The thought stuck in my mind. Boy, that makes all the difference in the world. Right there, that explained the difference between you and Mom, and it also explained what was lacking in my upbringing. Not that Mom didn't attempt to provide that love, but your explosive behavior countered everything she served up, except the food.

Meanwhile, with me in La-la Land, Mom was off and running, hardly camera-shy.

"So one day I was at the filling station. It was alongside

the road the presidents traveled on to get to the Black Hills. Well, this big black Packard pulls in. My father dashed inside and said, 'You'll never guess who's in the car?' He even gave Jerome a twenty-dollar tip. I asked my father, 'Who was it?' His eyes got real big and he said, 'Al Capone. It was Al Capone, and I saw him myself.' "

"Is that your Al Capone story?" I asked.

"I saw him myself." She nodded. "In that big black Packard. I'll never forget."

"You mean there was no shooting? No roughing anyone up? He wasn't bleeding?"

Mom shook her head.

"Was the Packard at least stolen?"

"I don't know, but it was expensive in those days," she said. "Now don't you want to ask me some more questions?"

I decided to be blunt and asked her about your drinking.

"Your daddy had a drinking problem," she said. "You know that. He would come home and supper would be ready and while the rest of us were eating, he'd have a quart of wine, which was a dollar a bottle. I'd say, 'Your dinner is ready,' and he'd say, 'I'll eat when I'm good and goddamn ready. When I feel like it.'

"He'd down the bottle, then come to the table, and by that time you kids would almost be done eating, and he'd gradually fall asleep. After a bit the boys would gradually lift him to the couch, and then he'd get up around ten and raise heck. I went through that a lot."

"It seems like you had more trouble with him than with the kids?"

"It was hard. But I'd keep saying, 'It'll get better.' "

"At least Dad always worked."

"He was a good worker, yes. As long as there was employment. But he was out of work a lot. I remember one time he went to the employment office and he was drawing thirty-eight dollars a week unemployment. We had all these kids and the guy there said to him with some disbelief, 'You know how many jobs you've had in the past year, Louie?' He'd had thirty-eight different jobs. That's because he'd work one day and then he wouldn't feel like going in again. He was tired."

"Well, what was it about Dad that attracted you to him, that made you stay with him and keep having children?"

"I loved him. Simple as that. I loved my husband. I came from a family where I didn't want for nothing. But we just made the best of it. Your daddy loved all you kids a lot. When we had the first four, he would bathe them and I would dress them and then he'd take them to band practice in Minneapolis. Later on, I think, he was just tired. Plain tired, and he drank.

"But when I first met him at the park over by Second Street, which I remember clear as anything, he was a handsome man, full of love. You know, Louie, I have no regrets over the choices I've made. Instead, I think I'm pretty lucky to be able to walk around at my age. You know I'm 135, don't you?"

I couldn't help but laugh in order to stop the lump that was growing in my throat. Mom's a talker, and the interview went on for ninety minutes. I have a feeling that it could've continued forever. It ended with her telling me about her own father, how he died of a stroke, but that it was really a broken heart resulting from loneliness. Mom mentioned that her own heart was strong and healthy.

"You know, I may have gone without a lot of luxuries," she finished. "But, kid, I'm getting them now. Every day."

Signed,

Time to interview myself

Dear Dad

Why don't I know you better?

I figure that you spent several hours a day for 40 years drinking. Multiply that by 365 days, then divide by 60 minutes, and then divide again by 24 hours. That's more than 1,000 days you spent with alcohol.

In other words, that's more than three years you spent with alcohol instead of your family.

I was alive for twenty-seven of those years, and I missed you.

Signed,
Counting the days

Dear Dad

I am at the airport, my home away from home, waiting to go through security. As I passed through the metal detector, I noticed a sign that read "Concealed weapons are against the law on planes." Or something like that. "By order of the FBI." In other words, don't bring concealed weapons onto the plane. My question is: What if you don't conceal them? What if you carry them out in the open?

"Hey, is that a machine gun?" the guard would ask.

"Yeah," I'd answer. "It's a machine gun. Best money can buy."

"What do you need it for?"

"Someone on the plane might be carrying a concealed weapon."

"Hand it over."

"Just kidding," I'd say. "It's a cigarette lighter."

"Wow, that's great," I can hear the guy saying. "Hey, man, check out this guy's cigarette lighter. Don't it look like a machine gun?"

As you well know, I'm not a neophyte when it comes to dealing with the FBI. Remember that knock on the door? Mom was in the kitchen with the water running. It always seemed to run for hours. Sometimes it was like she was waiting for something, letting the steady stream of water hit her hands as she rinsed a fork over and over. Maybe the water was her way out of the world we lived in. It was a cool shelter she could disappear into, a place that kept her mind off the chaos that always surrounded her.

Anyway, Mom didn't hear the door, and you were in the basement, trying to fix the washer. More than anything, I think, you loved to get out your tools and fix something, even if it worked. "Look at this," you'd say, running your hand along the needle-nosed pliers as if they were made of solid gold. "Did you ever see a pair of pliers like these?"

Maybe, just maybe, I'd think, they were different from the dozens of needle-nosed pliers in the hardware store. So I'd reach for them. But you'd snatch them away.

"And I don't ever want to see any of you kids touching them, either."

You never should've said that, Dad. I'd position Tommy by the drapes so he could monitor your departure for work. "Is he out of the driveway yet?" I'd ask. Tommy would nod, and I'd sprint down to the basement and take out each tool and run my hands over them. "I'm touching them," I'd squeal. "I'm touching them."

The knock at the door got louder, more impatient. I looked through the window and there were two nicely dressed men standing outside. Mormons, I thought, or the police. They sure weren't there to read the gas meter. I opened the door cautiously. "What do you want?" I asked.

"We want to talk to Louie Anderson," one of them said in a stern voice.

"I am Louie Anderson," I said.

They didn't seem to believe me.

"You were in World Wars One and Two?"

"Oh, you want my dad. Come in, and I'll get my mom. She'll find him."

I left them standing in the doorway, rushed to the kitchen, and tapped Mom on the shoulder. She jumped, startled, turned off the water, wiped her water-soaked hands off on her apron, and returned peacefully to this planet.

"Some men want Dad," I said.

"What men?" she asked.

"They're standing by the door."

I shrugged my shoulders, and Mom scurried to the basement door, called your name, and, without breaking stride, went into the living room. There was a sweet smile on her face, a smile she'd probably used more than a few times springing you from jams.

"Can I help you?" she chirped innocently.

"We're special agents, ma'am," they said by way of introduction. One agent reached into his coat and plucked out a small black leather wallet, opened it, and then uttered the three most important letters ever uttered in the Anderson household. "FBI."

I was frightened. Mom actually stumbled backward a step. Her smile vanished and was replaced by a look of concern. I thought I saw her glance back toward the sink, regretting that she'd ever removed herself from the reverie of the running water. I wondered what they wanted with us. Kent and Billy came to mind as possibilities. Then we heard your footsteps pounding on the basement steps, getting louder and louder, until you finally appeared in the doorway, a cigarette in your mouth, a wrench in your hand, and some serious questions in your eyes.

"Louie Anderson?" the agent asked again.

"Yes," you said.

"Can we ask you a few questions?"

I didn't suppose we had much choice. Everyone moved to a seat. The G-men were on the couch, you and Mom in chairs. As for me, I wouldn't have missed this scene for the world, but just in case anyone noticed me eavesdropping, I took a seat on the floor by the hallway to my room. If I was ordered out, I could leave quickly without too much embarrassment.

The bigger of the two agents took out a pad and pencil. "What, no gun?" I thought.

"Mr. Anderson," the other agent said as he, too, pulled something from his coat pocket. "Did you write this?"

I strained to see what it was. It looked like a Prizeword Pete postcard. You handled it like you'd never seen it before.

"Well," you stammered, "I was awful mad."

Your hands were shaking out of fear and nerves. I'd never seen you rattled before. It was a welcome sight, kind of. I was glad you were in trouble, but I was also mad at how they were talking to you. Even more frightening was that you were standing for it.

"Mr. Anderson," they said in a we're-not-kidding tone of voice, "you can't threaten the President of the United States."

You looked up from the postcard.

"Oh, for Christ sake, I was just mad. I didn't mean any of it."

This seemed like an apology, something I'd never heard pass your lips. At that moment I wanted to butt in and say that you also couldn't threaten your family. With the FBI there, maybe we could get some results. Put you in your place. I even entertained the idea of asking those gentlemen to stay a few years just to keep you in line. I wanted to blurt out, "And you know what else he does? He gets drunk and wakes me up at three A.M. He hits my mom. He calls us names and beats up the neighbor just because he has red hair."

Then I saw everyone was laughing. Damnit, you made them laugh. They weren't going to take you in. You had them in stitches, telling them about the wars, having eleven children, being poor, but still loving this country. I wanted to puke. Even more, I wanted to tell them that you were lying. I wanted to say, "He doesn't even like you guys. When you leave, he's going to swear at you." Then Mom offered coffee, a sign to either leave or take their coats off and stay. "Goodbye, Mr. Anderson," they said. "We're glad you're such a great American."

They thanked Mom for letting them inside, and then, adding insult to injury, they waved at me. "See ya, buddy."

"Am I in a dream?" I thought. Things were suddenly back to normal. Mom had the water running in the sink, and you were closing the front door.

"Christ, it's getting cold," you said. "I hope those assholes freeze to death. If their car doesn't start, I won't be helping them out. A couple of assholes, if you ask me. They're lucky I was in a half-decent mood."

With that, you sat down in your chair, picked up your rolling paper and tobacco, and stewed in a meditative silence. From then on you were mysteriously silent about

Nixon. But whenever he came on TV, you seemed interested in what he was saying, perhaps thinking that he was going to mention your name or that you'd be quizzed on it later.

Signed,

The other Louie Anderson

Dear Dad

It's ironic that a kid who quit high school would be asked back to give a motivational speech, but that's exactly the invitation I received the other day. I never felt much a part of any school I attended, high school most of all. My weight was the trouble. When you're fat, you're excluded from the various social groups. I think one of the reasons my joke about carrying a nine-by-twelve rug to nursery school goes over so well is that everyone carries some kind of burden in life.

In high school I was a hippie. I had long hair and did whatever I could to buck the norm. I was a radical looking for trouble. I once got in trouble for refusing to stand during the national anthem. I didn't do it because I had anything against the U.S. After all, my father was a veteran. I did it to irritate this one teacher who was a real stiff rod. That and my fondness for antagonizing authority.

This teacher was a real rigid goofball, and when I refused to stand, he hauled my butt down to the assistant principal's office and started to spew out this patriotic nonsense about his being a veteran who didn't risk his life so some anti-American commie punk like myself could desecrate the flag. That got me to spouting off about your being a disabled veteran. We yelled at each other for about fifteen minutes, while the assistant VP, a short, squat man with a bald head shaped like a nosecone, watched with his feet propped on his desk. When we finished yelling, he told us both to get out.

However, it was gym class that accelerated the end of my education. I hated, absolutely *hated*, gym class. Undressing my fat body in the locker room was the worst ego-shattering experience of my teenage life. If the kids weren't cracking jokes about my weight, they were staring at me. Some weren't as obvious as others. But I knew that they wanted to see what someone as fat as me looked like. It's the same way people look at someone who's missing a limb. People freak at anything that deviates from the norm. These days especially, they treat fat like a disease, like they'll catch it if they get too close.

While changing clothes, my heart would pound so hard waiting for the first giggle, trying to cover myself until I could get the undersized gym shorts on. I'd burn from embarrassment, feeling the blood flush my skin. Then I'd have to trot out onto the field, usually arriving late, where this sadistic little gym teacher with a big, bushy mustache and bowed legs would make me run and jump when all I wanted to do was hide.

The coach, as he liked to be called, always had this idea that he could take a guy who had been fat for ten years—me, for instance—and slim him down in ten months. I hated him for that, but I hated myself more.

It got to the point where I would do anything to get out of gym, including skipping the entire day of school. All I could think about was this one horrible hour. It filled me with so much fear and anxiety that I couldn't cope with the other hours in the day. As such, going to school became unbearable. Finally, I knew it had to end. I couldn't continue living with this stress. Then one day the twerp with the whistle roared the three words I dreaded.

"Take a lap!"

"Oh no, not laps," I thought.

I hated laps. I couldn't do them. I was fat. I smoked. I wasn't interested. I didn't want to do them. I'd walk.

"Pick it up, Anderson!" he'd shout. "Move it!"

"Screw him," I thought. And one day I just refused to do it.

"No," I thought, "I'm not going to run the lap."

Coach asked me what I was doing.

"I'm not going to run the lap," I explained calmly. "I can't, and you can't make me."

It wasn't very dramatic, at least as dramatic moments go, but the mini-mutiny I staged had a lasting effect on me. I was immediately ordered to get dressed and told to report to the chief gym czar, an even more demented, disagreeable fellow. I got dressed and walked out the door.

However, instead of going into the gym office, I turned the other way and walked right off the school grounds. "You know," I thought, "I'm never going to come back here."

Signed,

And I never did

Dear Dad

I've been thinking about what to say when I give my little pep talk at my old high school, and I've come up with two bits of wisdom.

1. Do your homework. Don't just learn to forge your mom's signature. Practice your dad's, too.
2. Don't run laps. Especially when they only serve to satisfy the ego of a demented gym teacher.

Signed,
Remembering the Three R's –
Rest, Relaxation, and Recess

Dear Dad

I was surprised when I came home and announced that I was quitting school and the roof didn't cave in. I told Mom, and she told you, and you mumbled a couple of comments. Truthfully, I think you knew it didn't matter what you said, my mind was made up. And really, what could you say? You didn't ever finish school and none of the boys graduated with their classes. You did have one thing to say, though.

"Just remember," you groused, "you'll have to get a job. You're not going to lay around here, goddamnit."

"Sure," I said, relieved that I would never have to run another lap again. "No problem."

What was I talking about? A job. Christ, I didn't have a job and I didn't want to work. Worse still, I had to go through the trouble of finding a job. I got a paper, scanned the want ads, and the next day landed a job at Shopper's City, a big department store where I was hired to unload boxes from trucks. After three hours on the loading dock, I asked my boss if he knew my gym teacher. If running laps was bad, this was a close second and nothing I wanted to endure.

So I quit.

I walked around town for the rest of the day, wondering what I'd tell everyone about my first day at work. Then, around quitting time, I went home and simply confesed that I'd turned in my hard hat. There had to be a way, I knew, to make money without sweating. There had to be. Not too long afterward, I got an idea. "I know," I thought. "I'll do what some of my brothers have done. I'll sell stuff."

Of course, what few people knew, and the fewer people who did know the better, was that the stuff I'd be selling was stolen.

However, fencing hot merchandise provided me with the lucrative career opportunity I hadn't previously thought about. One of my brothers was eager to set me up in the life that had made them famous among certain business associates. In fact, he was so enthusiastic with my interest that he spotted me some goods up front. They were ladies' clothes.

"What the hell am I going to do with them?" I said. "None of them fit me."

"Sell 'em to your friends' sisters," my brother said.

He had the process down pat. I'd sell the stuff for 50 percent of the list price. I'd keep 25 percent of that and give his suppliers 25 percent. It seemed like a fair arrangement.

After a while I got pretty good at it, too. I'd ask guys if their mothers or sisters needed any new clothes at a cut-rate price. They'd look at me funny, and I'd do some fast talking. It was a deal few could resist. The hours weren't bad. A little phone work, delivery at my convenience. There was just one problem. I wasn't making enough. I wanted more money. I mean, how many muu-muus can a guy sell?

You and Mom knew all about my criminal activities, which made me a bit uneasy, but nothing was ever said about it. It wasn't encouraged, but it wasn't discouraged, either. I understood your reasons. When you're poor, money is what you need, and where it comes from isn't high on the priority list. Plus, the whole family was so into denying reality that, if someone dealt with one issue, it was liable to cause a chain reaction of explosions.

Ambitious as I was, I started meeting other people who wanted me to sell stuff other than women's clothing. There was a lot more money involved, an incentive to any aspiring crook. This one group of guys I'd been introduced to stole a variety of goods, and one day they asked if I was interested in snowmobiles. I'd never thought of it, really. But what the hell, you know? I'd never thought of selling women's clothing. I had a lifestyle to support.

They also had a slick routine. People would go snowmobiling, and they'd stop at bars for a quick one to thaw them out. Because of the freezing cold, they'd leave their vehicles running outside the bars. Keys in the ignition and everything. Then these associates of mine would hop on them and take off. Easy as pie. They'd eventually drive the snowmobiles to my house and I'd put them in the garage. To sell them, I'd put out the word, and interested parties would stop by.

It was a good business to be in. Sales were brisk and the profit was good. I was climbing into the big bucks. Out-of-towners were my biggest customers. Unfortunately, like every criminal, I got careless and overconfident. I let a guy take one out and try to sell it on his own. I even gave him a pep talk. "No matter what," I said, "don't bring it back." But he did, and he brought the heat with him.

Not too long after he left, the doorbell rang. There were two guys in bad suits and overcoats standing outside.

"Is Louie Anderson here?" they asked.

"Yeah," I said, and then turned toward you. "Dad, it's for you!"

You lumbered into the room carrying a beer and a wrench.

"Are you Louie Anderson?" they asked.

"Yes," you said, puzzled.

"We're the police," they said, flashing their badges.

That's when I butted into the conversation.

"You probably want me. I'm also Louie Anderson."

"You have the right to remain silent," they said, repeating a line I'd heard too often on bad TV shows. "Anything you say can and will be used . . ."

I heard Mom gasp in the background. When I turned to see your reaction, I noticed that both of you had a look of dire concern. But especially Mom. One of her boys was being arrested right in her living room. I think she wanted to break the tension by offering everyone something to eat, but she was caught speechless.

I'll never forget the look on your face when the police asked us to go out to the garage. I couldn't recall you ever having paid so much fatherly attention to me. As bad as the situation was, it felt good to know that you were concerned for my welfare.

For some odd reason, I found the presence of the police a comfort. They had some authority over you that made me feel safer. It was snowing outside, so before we went out I asked if I could get a coat. The cops said okay, and I rushed into my bedroom, grabbed all the ladies' clothes I could hold, and called to Mom. "Where's my jacket?" I said.

She rushed in and I piled the clothes in her arms.

"Quick, put these in your closet when we go outside."

It was, I have to admit, exciting. I felt like a member of the Barker Gang.

"I can't find my coat," I said when I came back downstairs. "How cold is it?"

"Not bad," the big cop said.

The four of us walked outside—the two cops, me, and you. The snow crunched under our feet. I looked around for the landlord, the guy who owned the garage, but he wasn't around. The big cop had me open the garage, which I did, revealing a neat row of snowmobiles. No one said anything. The cops seemed content with looking at every little thing in the garage. "This yours?" the smaller, fatter cop asked, pointing at something.

"Only the snowmobiles are hot," I said. "The rest belongs to the guy who owns the house."

They peered into my eyes, questioning the validity of my last statement.

"Ask him, if you don't believe me."

They peered at me again, long and hard, using that special vision radar police seem to possess. Then they pointed to the car that was parked there.

"This yours, too?"

I couldn't believe someone would actually question the ownership of a beat-up, 1961 Chevy station wagon. I wanted to say, "No, I'm filling a special order, and I had to look forever to come up with this jalopy." But I bit my tongue. Who knew what was going to happen to me. I could've been looking at ten to twenty years' hard labor for my misdeeds, all for not being able to run laps in gym class.

The cops escorted me back to the front, where their brown sedan was parked on the wrong side of the street. Did you ever notice how many traffic laws police violate for no apparent reason? U-turns, parking in red zones, speeding. They get away with everything but murder. A few words were exchanged, and then we left you at the front door. Your parting words to me were "Tell them the truth." I nodded my head obediently, but inside I was thinking, "Since when do we do that in our family?" The trip to the station house took fifteen minutes. They uncuffed my hands and I was fingerprinted and photographed. I think they planned an interrogation, but before the guy could finish the first question, I confessed everything. I spilled my guts. The biggest stool pigeon ever to sit on a stool. It all happened so fast that I had little time to think about the gravity of the situation. A court date was set and I was released, a sixteen-year-old con with a bleak future. I was out of school, out of work, and out of luck.

Signed,

Brother, can you spare a dime?

Dear Dad

In retrospect, the jolt I received by crashing headfirst into the long arm of the law was exactly what I needed to give some direction to my confused adolescence. The Justice Department spun me around, inadvertently set my life in order and gave me a second chance to prove myself. Secretly, I basked in the attention I received by getting in trouble. For a change, it was nice to be the focus of everyone's concern, even if I did have to go before a judge to get it.

As a first-time offender, however, I was given six months' probation, not a bad deal considering what the cops found me holding, and a probation officer. His name was Lyle Christenson, a gentle Scandinavian man who became a savior in disguise. He was the first adult male to take a serious interest in my welfare and future. Lyle was really concerned about me. He listened when I talked, laughed when I made a joke, and responded when I expressed fear. He also dispensed advice that had only my best interest in mind. To me, it was a unique relationship.

Looking back, I realize how important it was to have someone caring about me, prodding me to make something of myself, and making me give of myself as much as I took from others. It's called "restitution" in the legal world. In my situation, it was more a case of emotional stability. Lyle convinced me to return to school. "Got to get your degree," he'd constantly say. The thing is, I believed him. I re-enrolled at Johnson High, a newly motivated eleventh-grader, who attended class all day and then again for three hours at night to make up for the year that I'd missed. The prize was graduating with my class.

Did I mention that I was invited back to school to give a speech? I finally got around to investigating the offer and it turns out that they want to honor me as the most successful graduate of Johnson High. It's a delicious irony, but the truth is, I feel like I have something to say to those kids.

I've always thought that I've had all the answers to the truly big questions in life. Parents should love their children. Children should enjoy being young. The things that taste the best are always the worst for your health and should be eaten in moderation except in times of extreme anxiety. And women should be in charge of everything. If they were, hunger and the homeless problems would be taken care of. Priorities would be hot meals and clean clothes. Drug-related crimes would probably ebb, too.

As it is now, the cops show up at a crack house, there's a shootout or a mass arrest, people die or get thrown into overcrowded jails, they're released a few weeks later, and the cycle continues unbroken. But imagine a knock on the door and the dealer sliding back the secret panel. "Oh shit!" he says. "It's my mom." He'd have to let her in, and she'd take care of the situation.

"Are you on drugs?" she'd say.

"No."

"Don't lie to me. I'm your mother."

"Yes, Mom. I'm on drugs."

"Well, we're just going to do something about that, and we're going to do it right now."

"Now?"

"Right now, young man," she'd snap, "and I don't want to hear any backtalk. You're living in a pigsty, and you're wasting your money. Now, we're just going to clean up this filth, then get you into a bath and some clean clothes, and find you a job. And we're going to do this all before your father gets home from work, because he's worked hard and doesn't deserve to be upset. Do you hear me?"

I can imagine the other addicts watching this and thinking, "Shit, I'm getting outta here before she tells my mom."

It's a cruel world, which is, sadly, an overused cliché that's true, but only because there isn't enough caring and love. I truly believe that, and I know it from firsthand experience. After graduating, I went to work as a volunteer parole officer under my friend Lyle. Perhaps I was cozying up to him, searching for the paternal affection from this surrogate father that I didn't get at home. But I actually felt that, because of what I'd been through, I had something to offer other kids.

"A few months later I took a bigger job in St. Paul, at the Arlington House for Boys, a treatment center for wayward and abused kids that was run by an extremely religious man. He believed God was the answer to every problem that walked through the door. I consider myself a spiritual person, but, honestly, I didn't see God helping these kids who came in bruised and battered by their parents. There was finally a big showdown, and I quit.

I think I took my next job to get back at that pious old man who ran Arlington House. In fancy terms, I was a telephone solicitor, but actually I was a fast-talking pitchman selling advertising space in a prayer book called *The Catholic Devotional*. The job was a bit on the shady side. About eight of us sat at desks in a small, stuffy office above a beauty salon, where we dialed businesses across the country, trying to convince them that we were with the local Catholic church.

The guy who ran it always had a cigarette in his hand, slicked-back hair, and he loved to play gin rummy and pick up the mail. Both pastimes involved money. He'd patrol our work spaces, monitoring out phone pitches, encouraging us to lather on the sweet talk and "bring home the bacon." I still remember my pitch.

"Hi, this is Louie Anderson with *The Catholic Devotional.*"

Then I'd usually hear the "click" of a hangup. I'd call the next one. I nearly fell off my chair the first time someone didn't slam down the receiver.

"Yes?" he said.

"Ah yes," I stammered, not used to anyone responding. "This is our prayer book that's distributed free to all Catholic churches in the area, and I was wondering if we might run this little ad for you. It would read 'Paul's Hardware and Appliances' in large bold type. And beneath that we'll insert your location and telephone number."

He was still on the line.

"May I set this up for you, sir?"

"How much?" he asked.

Numbers ran through my head: $27, $48, $72, or $96. I didn't know.

"Oh Christ, it's my first day," I said, flipping through my instruction booklet. "It's only twenty-seven dollars for a full year."

"Okay, I'll take it."

"He said okay," I told my boss, cupping the receiver. "He wants it. What now?"

"Get his name."

"Yes sir, well, could I get your name, please? Paul, of course. Paul's Hardware. And I have your address, too. Well, thank you, Paul."

I was so excited. My first sale. Eventually, I got pretty good at the business. But I knew all along the operation was fairly shady. I didn't last quite a year. One day a priest paid a surprise visit to the boss and left without saying goodbye, which I took as my cue to scram. After all, I didn't want my old pals in blue who knew me from my snowmobiling days to see me here. I was trying to make something of myself.

Signed,

Onward and upward

Dear Dad

By eighteen years of age, I had devised what I call "Louie's Rules to Live By."

1. Tell the truth.
2. It's okay to cry.
3. It's even better to hug someone.
4. Failure is nothing to fear as long as you try.
5. Don't be afraid to say "I love you."

Of course, these aren't the same as "Louie's Rules of Survival." They are a bit different.

1. Don't speak unless you can cause conflict.
2. Yell at everyone except the person who needs it.
3. Lie about everything, like everyone else.
4. Try to find self-worth wherever you can.
5. Say "I love you" to everyone, even if you don't mean it.

Signed,
You were the inspiration

Dear Dad

You alone ruined me as far as day jobs go. Always waking up at 3:00 A.M., I eventually became a night person. The St. Joe's Home for Children in Minneapolis was looking for a night person about the time I realized this and decided that I should find work during those hours. The unit where I worked, an emergency ward for neglected, abused kids and runaways, was called Shelter Three, and by the looks of things it was the last place anyone would expect to find love.

But it's where I found it.

In the sad eyes and weary, bruised faces of the children I was assigned to watch over, I found an aching emptiness that was similar to what I felt in my own heart. I understood their silence, their refusal to cry, and when they did cry or wake from bad dreams, I could honestly tell them, "I understand."

Naturally, the job wasn't easy. The kids were constantly testing me. As the night person, it was my job to put them to bed, and for them bedtime was the hardest. They were all kids who were afraid of what might happen to them when they closed their eyes, afraid of what went on in the darkness. So, as soon as the lights went off, they would start in. A door would open, then slam, then open and slam again. There'd be giggles, nervous, playful giggles. I'd ignore it at first. But it would get louder.

"Fuck you!"

"No, fuck you!"

That would do it. They'd hear my tennis shoes squeaking on the floor as I walked down the hall and they'd quiet down. Sometimes I'd fool them by removing my shoes and sneaking down in my stocking feet. I'd push open the door and shine the flashlight in their faces.

"Busted!" I'd laugh, waiting for one of their many excuses.

"Well . . . I . . . uh," they'd stammer. "Could I use the bathroom?"

"No," I'd snap, trying to preserve my authority. "And don't wet the bed, either. It's electrified."

Humor helped a lot with these kids. They rarely had cause to laugh. One time a kid went berserk in the lounge. He clutched a fork and threatened to kill everyone in the place. I walked in and offered to help him.

"Why do you want to fork everyone over?" I asked. "Have you been forked over yourself?"

He laughed. We all did, and he put the fork down and we processed it out. That's institutional talk for hashing and rehashing the incident, over and over again, until you've convinced the kid that he was wrong and you were right. "Next time," I told him, "use a plastic fork."

The place was full of sad stories. I'd read the files while everyone slept and feel my heart break. But the files were nothing compared to real life. One night, around 3:00 A.M., this little girl with big brown eyes was brought in. Before I could put her to bed, I had to go through the admitting procedure, which began with a series of routine questions. How old are you? Where do you live? Where do you go to school? Blah, blah, blah.

Then I asked, "Why did you come here?"

"I don't know," she said quietly.

"Well, what happened tonight?"

"Nothing."

"You just woke up and said, 'I think I'll go to St. Joe's Home for Children in the middle of the night.' "

She was silent and I let it sink in.

"I won't hurt you," I said.

She raised her eyes from the spot on the floor where she'd been staring and looked directly into my eyes. She was judging me, deciding whether or not to trust me.

"My parents," she said, stopping to stave off the tears that were welling in her eyes. "My parents were fighting, and the police came and took me away."

"What were they fighting about?"

"My dad was drinking, and he gets mad when he drinks. Then he yells and throws things and hits my mom. Sometimes he hits my sister, and I have to protect her. So I hit him. Then he really got mad, and he said he was going to kill me. When he said that, my mom got a pan and hit him, and he went crazy. Then the police came and brought me here."

Moments like those make you realize how brave children are and how cowardly adults can be. I got up from the desk and took her hand.

"Let's get you settled in a room," I said.

Holding her hand, I led her to the closet, where I gave her a blanket, sheet, and pillow. Then I took her to a small room, told her the schedule for the morning, and said good night. As I began shutting the door, I heard a tiny, frail whisper.

"Could you please leave the light on?" she asked.

I started to say no, but caught myself and said, "Sure, I will. Have a good sleep."

I went from there into the staff bathroom and over to the sink, where I turned on the cold water and stared into the mirror. Tears were streaming down my face. I was shaken. Her story wasn't my story. But part of it was. Right then I realized what it meant to be human and just how precious and fragile is the flowering of a young life. I took a deep breath, splashed cold water on my face, and went to the snack closet, where we hid the candy.

Signed,

Where's the punchline?

Dear Dad

After that I never felt much like working at St. Joe's. It wasn't what I wanted to do, I realized, but I had nowhere else to go. So I worked hard and climbed their ladder, getting promoted from nights to days and from days to lead child-care worker to supervisor of the entire unit. It was pretty good for a guy with only a high-school education.

My asset was that I understood kids, and something inside me made me care about them, despite not wanting to work there. I stayed at the job three years, but it did get tiring. The system did nothing but perpetuate itself. The same kids would come in time after time. They'd arrive at St. Joe's, return to their families for a while, and, soon enough, the same problems would come up again and back they'd come. Usually till they moved on to the next system.

Strangely, they didn't mind coming back, because, I realized, we provided a better family situation than they had at home. Come to think of it, that's why I stuck around, too. It became my surrogate family. I knew everyone, loved seeing them and socializing with them after work. The downside is that I began to drink myself.

I wasn't the only one, though. Lots of the people who worked there drank. Maybe drowning and numbing the sorrowful sights we dealt with daily was the only way we could get ourselves to return again. But a routine developed. After our three-to-eleven shift, a bunch of us would meet at the bar. At first I only drank sodas. But it looked like everyone who drank was having such a great time. You never sang and danced or wrapped your arm around my shoulder and told me what a great guy I was, but that's what we did at the bar. And after the bar closed, we'd buy more beer and take it down to the lake and get even drunker.

After these ordeals, we'd usually all end up at some greasy-spoon diner, eating and trying to sober up. I enjoyed this, especially the tightly knit camaraderie, but I realized the drinking would lead me to trouble if I didn't cool it, and the one thing I didn't want was to turn out like you. So, after getting drunk one evening and telling off this loud-mouth goofball for no good reason I can recall, I decided to quit. I never drank again. It was like a buzzer went off in my head. I didn't want to become another drunken Anderson.

I still went out with the gang, and one night we decided to try a favorite bar. They wanted two dollars to get inside.

"For what?" I asked. "It didn't used to be like this."

"Comedy night," a big bouncer said.

"We don't want comedy," I said. "We're regulars. Where's Larry, the guy who's usually here?"

"He's off tonight. Two bucks or you can't get in."

"Screw that," I said. "Let's go."

But my friend O'Brien interjected and said he'd pay.

"Okay, you pay," I said, "and I'll laugh."

The bar was small, even smaller with a makeshift stage, and the chairs and tables were stacked practically on top of each other. The guy onstage was a beefy Italian who was doing a Popeye the Sailor impression. Then another comic did his stuff. "These guys aren't funny," I told O'Brien. "I can't believe we had to pay for this garbage. I'm funnier than this in my sleep."

"If you think you're so funny," he said, "why don't you go up there and try it?"

"Maybe I will," I said.

I wanted to talk and he wanted to listen to the comics. Finally, I gave in and listened, too. Like a good boy, I sat back and paid attention, and discovered that this one guy wasn't bad. But I didn't want to admit it, not after putting everyone down. As we watched some more, I even found myself laughing along with the rest of the crowd.

"It's too bad you don't like any of these guys," O'Brien said.

When the show was finished, I went up to one of the comedians I liked and introduced myself. "You were great," I said. "How does a guy get into this?"

"Every Friday we play at Mickey Finn's," he said. "You know it?"

"Yeah. Can anyone do it?"

"If you're funny."

"I'll be down Friday," I said, automatically judging myself funny.

"Okay," he said.

"Do I need to call anyone?"

"Just come down and bring lots of friends," he said. "We need an audience."

He returned to packing up the microphone and I went over and told O'Brien what I was going to do the following Friday.

"You're what?" he said incredulously.

"Well, you dared me."

I gave the comics a wave as they left.

"See you Friday," I called.

They gave me a fake smile, like, Sure, we'll see you. I already felt different. Terrified, in fact. What was I going to talk about?

Signed,

But seriously, folks

Dear Dad

It was my debut. I told the jokes, but, Dad, you delivered the zinger.

The date was October 10, 1978, and the place was Mickey Finn's, the little club the comic had told me about. I'd always known I was funny. From boyhood on, I had a talent for articulating injustice. But I'd never considered myself humorous in a professional way. My comedic debut was nothing more than living up to a dare.

I worked all week on my jokes, my fat jokes, and to insure that I went over well, I packed the audience with all my pals from the children's home and anyone else I could think of who was free that evening. You and Mom were there, too. I was frightened at first. My left leg, I remember, was shaking as if a vibrator was stuck in my sock. I don't think anyone else noticed, but I still pointed it out to everyone. "Look at my leg shaking," I said.

Then it was over. I walked off the stage and was congratulated by everyone. What else were they going to say? These were all my closest friends and relatives. Secretly, though, I knew that comedy was going to be my new career. It was love at first laugh.

Unfortunately, by morning it all seemed like a too distant dream. Mom called early.

"Louie, your dad had a stroke," she said.

She told me you were at the VA hospital. Instantly, I

blamed myself for what happened to you. The excitement, I thought, was too much for you. I told Mom I'd be there as soon as possible, then tried to make a joke.

"I wanted to knock 'em dead," I said, "but I didn't mean to hurt anyone."

Signed,

Feeling guilty

Dear Dad

I'm lying in bed, recuperating from my first brush with death. In the beginning, I thought it was food poisoning. The last time I felt this ill I went to the hospital, they gave me some medicine, and the pain vanished. But not this time. It continued for hours, long into the night, and as I rolled around on the bed, I realized it wasn't going to get any better.

My initial diagnosis was simply too much food. Maybe I'd overeaten. I'd gone out for Thai food, then cherry pie, and then I'd snacked on some fruit salad when I got back home. Indigestion, I thought. But when that didn't let up, I knew it had to be food poisoning.

By 4:00 A.M., though, I decided to go to the hospital. The pain had increased and was constant. I couldn't straighten up. I could hardly walk. Nonetheless, I decided that I was still in good enough shape to drive myself across town to the hospital. I didn't want the fuss of an ambulance. Nor could I see two guys hoisting me up into the back of a meat wagon.

I pulled on my sweatpants and slipped on a jacket. I didn't bother with a shirt; I wasn't making a fashion statement. Looking like hell, which is where I thought my next stop might be, I walked down all fifty-four stairs doubled over like Charles Laughton in *The Hunchback of Notre Dame*, climbed in my car, and began the trek to the hospital. I drove slowly, thinking that, if I was dying, I didn't want to get into an accident.

A few people were already going to work. At one red light I saw a guy in his pickup truck drinking coffee out of one of these no-spill cups. No matter what, I thought, people always look silly using those cups. They remind me of the cups babies get when they're first learning to drink out of a glass. "Maybe there's a joke there," I remember thinking then. Then I caught myself. There I was, dying, and trying to write new material. But why stop and take life seriously just because I was dying?

There were only a few cars in the parking lot when I pulled in to the hospital. I wanted to stop right in front of the emergency-room entrance, but those spaces were all reserved. What if I lived? I didn't want someone to yell at me for parking in the wrong spot. And if I died, I didn't want to leave a ticket on my car. I finally hobbled up to the door, where one of the security guards made like he recognized me. I saw his eyes light up, and for a second I thought he was going to ask for an autograph. But I shot him a glance that indicated I wasn't making a promotional appearance.

With a great deal of relief, I made it up to the front desk. Of course, no one was around. I heard a woman in the waiting area moan, "I'm dying. I'm dying. Please, someone, help me." I thought, "Lady, I know just how you feel." Just then, a big, menacing nurse appeared at the window and asked if she could help me.

"Yes," I said, "I have a pain in my stomach."

She peered through the window at my abdomen, which was throbbing so hard with pain I wondered if she couldn't see it. But she seemed nonplussed and gave me a so-who-doesn't-have-pain look. Suddenly, I felt guilty. Maybe I wasn't sick enough. Maybe I needed an open vein to be spurting blood everywhere.

"You got insurance?" she asked.

I nodded.

"Good, then sit down next to that woman and fill out these papers."

Finally, I persuaded the nurse that I could afford to be sick, which made all the difference in the world. From behind bullet-proof glass, she took my insurance information and an imprint of my American Express card, and then she called an orderly, who whisked me down the hall. I heard the old woman in the lounge moan even louder. "I'm dying," she rasped, probably pissed off they took me ahead of her.

I was deposited on an empty bed in a bright room. The orderly pulled the large curtain around me. Privacy, I thought. But I was wrong. A closed curtain seemed to be a magnet, attracting the attention of every single person who walked by. They'd stick their head in, look at me, and mutter, "Oh." I was in too much pain to lay down, so I just stood there, bent over. I wonder, though, if everyone looks over at that counter full of stuff and thinks, "Okay, what can I steal? Do I need ten thousand feet of gauze tape?" They're going to charge you for it all anyway.

My criminal mind was going full-speed when the nurse Helga appeared, handed me this gown about the size of a handkerchief, and told me to slip it on. Right. I wanted to ask for two of them. But I decided to just comply and let medical science run its course. The pain was getting worse, and apparently they'd moved the old woman nearby, because her moaning was getting louder and louder. "I'm dying!"

I was getting ready to join the chant. As I tried to lay down with my ass hanging out of the tiny hospital gown, I started thinking of you, Dad. All those times I saw you in a hospital bed, tubes in your nose, a faint smile on your face, a sense of strength and fight in your heart. You never complained and always remained hopeful. I was off in that world, just staring out into space, mulling the complicated questions of life and death, nearly forgetting the shooting pain, when a doctor came in, all smiles and cheer.

He asked me to roll over on my back, and then he started poking. As he was doing this, I gave him my expert opinion on the food-poisoning angle. "We're going to run some tests and take some blood," he said, ignoring my diagnosis. I knew what that meant. I was going to be in pain a little longer. "We'll see what comes up," he intoned.

I hate when they take blood. They can never find the vein and the guy who does it always looks like he just woke up. As for me, the man who hates needles, I'd already turned white. The expression on my face resembled a sick Pekingese. Like always, the guy poked and prodded and finally found the vein. After the fourth vial, pain or no pain, I complained. "Hey, how much do you need? Does someone need a transfusion?"

Shortly after he left, Nurse Helga returned with an IV setup. She explained that it would be hooked up to the back of my hand.

"Oh no," I said, worried, "nothing's supposed to go there."

"Just a little prick," she said after dabbing a spot with alcohol.

It burned when she put it in. I jerked, and she quickly taped it down. Finally, after seeing the doctor a few more times, I was able to convince him that I needed something for the pain. He told Helga to give me four or five cc's of morphine.

"Yes, there is a God," I thought. "Morphine is exactly what I need."

Just thinking about it made me feel better. I wanted to thank the doctor, but realized it wasn't appropriate. Then I was hit by a wave of guilt. There were others in the world who were suffering more severe pain than I was; maybe I didn't need it. The hell I didn't, I convinced myself as Helga injected the drug into the IV tube.

A few seconds later, things were becoming clearer. The pain was leaving, or so my mind thought.

Is this what alcohol did for you at first? Numb the pain? After a while, of course, it only caused you and everyone else pain. But I think I can guess what it might've done for you.

Because, in a matter of minutes, the morphine had kicked in. I felt better. I wanted to talk to everyone. My emotions were overwhelming, free, and everything was beautiful.

"Doc," I mumbled, "if you need to open me up, go ahead and do it right here. Everything's okay. I don't want to be a problem."

He flashed me an understanding smile, as though he knew that I'd lost my mind.

"I love you," I told him.

He didn't even look up. The nurse took my pulse.

"I love you, too," I told her.

She didn't notice, either. It didn't matter. I was suddenly in love with everyone. I heard the moaning again, this time right next to me. I opened my curtain, leaned out, and opened the curtain surrounding the bed next to mine. "Are you still dying?" I said. There was the old woman. She looked at me, tried to smile, and then shook her head yes. "Well, then, get some morphine," I told her. "I was dying, and now I'm cured."

Signed,

I'm on morphine

Dear Dad

What an education! In the brief span of one week I learned all about death, love, and gallstones. On a serious note, though, I took that rather grim experience as a sign from above that I needed to perform an abrupt about-face with my life. Clean up. Kick the food. Get beyond my emotional hangups. Make a clean break with the past.

In surfer lingo, I needed to "go for it." It was time to stop merely thinking about changing my life and actually take the steps.

Without realizing it, however, I'd begun doing just that months earlier when I'd started the tedious process of editing the family videotape I'd shot way back over Christmas. I'd watched the reels over and over again, never in sequence, touched by the intense and revealing intimacy expressed so eloquently in simple terms. Yet after a few viewings I also began to look at the tapes with the detached eye of a performer.

There was something there that related directly to my performance. I couldn't put my finger on it, but it was there. How could I use this, I wondered?

When my strength returned, I rented space in an editing room and began piecing together a single videotape from the hours of interviews I had collected. I began with Mom talking about where she was from and the birth of your first child. "My oldest boy, Kent, was born at home," she said.

"We didn't have a crib, so he slept in the top drawer of the dresser."

Then I cut to Kent. "The sad memories are insignificant compared to the happy ones," he started off. "A family like ours made us unconcerned with success the way the world measures it. We don't care what people think of us or if we fit in. The good thing about our life is, it made us reasonably creative and self-sufficient."

As the oldest, Kent's comments were particularly insightful, but I liked a short vignette Rhea told enough to put it up front. "Dad would stop in the alley, where there was a big apple tree," she said. "He would say, 'Now, when I stop the truck, you shake the tree.' We would shake it and the apples would fall into the truck. He was really clever."

Getting a rough cut assembled took several days, but it was tough deciding what to put in and what to leave out. The things people chose to remember were moving. "He always loved his cars," Jim added. "He would go out in the cold and put a blanket on them." One thing's for sure: not everything I put in was complimentary, no, not by any means. Honesty was the bottom line. "I think Dad was a crazy man," Mary said. "He was very unhappy, and the worst thing about him was his drinking." In many instances, the anger came across as still raw and unrequited. "I think we made our own happiness, but I don't think we were a happy family," Lisa offered. "I think the Anderson family should try to love each other more. Just because Dad didn't take the time with us, doesn't mean that we shouldn't take the time now."

Ending the piece was especially difficult. I led in with me asking Mary what it was like when you played the trumpet.

"It was wonderful," she said. "It was like he was a star."

Then I asked Lisa what would be the one thing she'd say to you, given the chance.

"If I could say one thing to Dad," she thought, "I'd say, 'You left too soon.' "

Finally, I ended with Roger declaring, "Dad, I wouldn't have changed you for any other dad in the world, drinking or not."

The last image was a photo of you. Your glasses seemed about ready to slide down the bridge of your nose. When that picture was taken, Mom had told me, she'd had to practically beg you to take off your hat. "I thought he was so handsome," she'd said. I agree. You looked good for an old man.

I repeated Roger's last sentence over and over, listening to it in the dark little room lit only by the light from your illuminated photo.

Signed,

Wondering if I'll be able to say that

Dear Dad

Among other things I received in this morning's mail was a letter from Mom containing a letter that I had written to her seven years ago. It was dated October 10, 1982, and must've been immediately prior to a barnstorm tour of small clubs I was embarking on in a beat-up, borrowed Chevy. It started:

Hi. Really enjoyed talking with you on the phone. It sounds like things are going well. I am concerned about getting to Denver. I could use $100 that I could pay right back after I get to Kansas City, which is the 27th. If you can help me out, it would pay for my gas to get there. Let me know. I want to leave Monday, October 18th.

I am still doing O.K. I have my rent paid for this month and it looks O.K. til the 1st of the year. I know I will make it. It's just a matter of time. Take care.

Making the leap into comedy full-time wasn't as difficult a decision as it might seem. First off, I was tired of working with kids who wouldn't listen, tired of battling parents who wouldn't change, and exhausted from dealing with a system that wasn't interested in making the radical changes necessary to improve the dire needs of the people it was serving. Even more important, however, people at the comedy club were asking for me, phoning Mickey Finn's to see if I was scheduled to perform.

I can't complain about the star treatment I get these days when I play in Las Vegas or Atlantic City, but some of my favorite memories are of walking into that little club during the afternoon and readying it for a show. We'd move the chairs and tables around to make the most of the seating, taking a big, long piece of plywood and setting it over milk crates. We'd hook up the old sound system and set the microphone up. And we'd remove all the salt and pepper shakers, because we didn't want food to be served while we were performing.

Dad, it was during these moments that I related to you most as a performer. I'd try to imagine you traveling by train from city to city, setting up before a performance, and winding down at night afterward. I hated to admit it, but I was having fun. I knew you must've had fun playing your horn, sitting on the bandstand and leaning back to hit that high C and feeling so damn proud after because it was strong and loud and clear. In later years maybe you found that same feeling in a bottle. But I wish we could've traveled together.

Anyway, soon after leaving St. Joe's I went to St. Louis for the First Annual Comedy Competition. It was hosted by Henny Youngman. Even then I didn't like this sort of competition. There's one winner and the rest are losers. I've never felt that anyone who puts forth effort should be called a loser.

There were ten comics competing, and I can still clearly visualize all of us standing around the back room, smiling, subtly trying to psych each other out. The contest was being held in a hotel ballroom. There were twelve hundred people in the audience, the biggest crowd I'd ever played to. I remember it was oddly quiet, too. All of us paced back and forth, trying to contain our pre-contest nerves. Then Henny Youngman entered the room. We all stared at him, a star. A telephone rang and, without missing a beat, he quipped, "If that's my manager, get his name."

I laughed hard, though now I wonder if he'd planned that scene. It didn't matter. He greeted us and we praised him. He sat with his violin and spewed one-liners and we asked him questions that enabled him to tell one show-business story after another. He talked about Hope, Berle, Burns, and Benny. But mostly we heard about him.

After the host announced that the show was nearly set to start, we drew numbers to determine the order of appearances. A black guy from St. Louis drew the opening spot. A girl impressionist I knew from Minneapolis got number seven. A juggler from Kansas City picked three. The guy from Chicago who sang funny songs selected number six, a prime spot. Me, I picked number ten. Dead last. "Oh well, best for last," someone said with a grin that let me know he thought it was better me than him. I returned his smile and wondered if anyone in the audience would be left by then.

I needed to get out of there. Go for a walk. Breathe. I really wanted to get something to eat, to calm my nerves by filling my stomach, but I decided to save that reward for afterward. I wandered in and out, returning before the finish of each act so I could hear the response. Two were out of it, I could tell. They were too nervous. But the guy who played songs was really on. He'd win, I thought, though he shouldn't have been allowed to compete at all. This was comedy, not a music festival.

I walked into the hotel lobby, smiling at the desk clerks. "I'm tenth," I blurted out.

They looked at me like I was insane. I explained that I was tenth in the contest.

"Oh, is that tonight?" one of them asked.

I couldn't believe it. Their lives didn't revolve around my comedy career?

"Have people been leaving?" I asked.

"No, not that I know of."

"Good, let's hope they don't. I'm tenth."

I wandered back in. Three more people, then my turn. The juggler and the guitar player, I figured, were both possible winners, and, fortunately, there were no more sideshow acts. But the show was beginning to drag, and I spotted a few people in the crowd yawning. The emcee was doing too much time between acts. I said something to him about it, which only irritated him and made him talk even longer the next time, just to show me who was boss.

After what seemed an eternity, I was finally introduced. I fired off all my fat jokes with as much confidence and speed as possible, trying to build momentum. Wrapping it up, I asked the piano to start a lightly played rendition of "All of Me," over which I closed with my surest material. It was a weak attempt at a Vegasy ending, but the audience cheered. Even Henny Youngman was standing up. I thought, "Maybe I could win."

Backstage, the comics and the emcee treated me with a renewed respect as I strutted by them. Naturally, though, on my way past them, I tripped on the carpet. It was God's way of bringing me back to earth, of reminding me that I was human. No problem, though. I'd done okay. Henny Youngman performed a brief set while the scoring was completed, and then it was the emcee's big moment.

"And the moment you've all been waiting for," he began, drawing it out, knowing he'd go back to being a little fish in a big pond once this was completed. "The winner of the First Annual Comedy Competition . . . Before that, can we have another round of applause for Henny Youngman . . . The winner, from Chicago . . ."

I knew it. The guitar player won. Second went to the juggler. "And third place," he drawled, "or third banana, goes to Louie Anderson from Minneapolis, Minnesota."

I wasn't a sore loser, but as I walked out to take a bow, I thought, "Oh Christ, I was much better than them." But at least I got third. Henny Youngman presented the plastic banana trophies to us, and as he handed mine to me, he whispered, "You were the best. You should've won." He didn't know it, but what he said was worth all the bananas in the world.

Signed,

Take my jokes, please

Dear Dad

I've got an idea on how to use the videotape. Show it during a portion of my act. It'll let the audience see where the comedy comes from. Granted the premise is a bit radical, but interesting as a real creative departure.

The idea hit me the other week after I was interviewed by *People* magazine for a story about children of alcoholics. My career was neatly summarized in several sentences. "He began performing at a local comedy club, then moved six years ago to L.A., where he became a regular at the Comedy Store and made his debut on the *Tonight* show in 1984. He is co-starring in a feature film, *The Wrong Guys*, and is producing *The Johnsons Are Home*, a TV sitcom based on his own family."

Then the story went on to talk about real issues, like your drinking and its effects on our family and on me, and how I learned to deal with these things by telling jokes. I was impressed with the article's effort to focus on the substance of a person's life. Not their accomplishments, but what in their lives made them want to achieve.

I liked being written about as a real person and not an entertainer. I always hate it when celebrities are made to seem like God's gift. I hate it most when they're described as geniuses. Geniuses discover vaccines; they don't tell jokes.

Anyway, it got me wondering if the same thing might work with the video onstage. If I could not only tell the audience jokes, but show them where they came from.

Signed,

What do you think?

Dear Dad

Yesterday I received this letter in the mail from one of my brother's sons.

Dear Louie,

I read the article in *People* magazine about your father and how his alcoholism affected you. It helped me understand my relationship with my father. I want desperately to speak to him about it, but he seems unapproachable. I hope I can talk to him before he dies.

> Love,
> Your nephew

The letter made me cry.

> Signed,
> *I know how you feel*

Dear Dad

Twenty minutes. Only twenty minutes more. That's how much longer I have to stay on this treadmill. I'm thinking "downhill." You know, it's difficult to write and walk at the same time, but I don't want to interrupt my training routine. I walk every day for one hour. I've been doing it for a month. Me, the kid who quit school over running laps. I walk and walk and walk and walk, until the sweat is pouring out and I'm panting like a dog who's run across country in search of his master after taking a wrong turn at the end of the driveway.

I walk and walk and walk and, even though I've put in enough miles to go from Los Angeles to London, I never move an inch. It's the worst kind of exercise. Boring, painful, agonizing, and boring. But as I chalk up the miles, I imagine that I'm moving farther away from death, and I feel better for it.

Everyone, I think, tries to keep a safe distance from death. Some are more open about it than others. They jog, work out, maintain vegetarian diets, vacation at health spas, get their faces lifted and their fat sucked out and their butts tucked, and they talk endlessly about the difference between good and bad cholesterol. The rest smoke and drink and continue to gobble up red meat, figuring that, if they simply don't think about death, it'll ignore them, too.

So the proper diet and exercise will add a year or two

extra. Big deal. After eighty, what's the difference? Then all anyone really cares about is being able to walk on your own and go to the bathroom by yourself.

Either way, everyone succumbs at the end. That's the punchline to the big mystery of life. We don't know why we're here, yet we don't want to leave, either.

Dad, you fell into the latter category, except you were one hell of a fighter. You beat the emergency appendectomy. You beat the stroke. You outlasted your drinking and beloved unfiltered Bull Durhams. The only opponent you couldn't beat was the big C. Cancer. But you didn't go easy, that's for damn sure.

I was sound asleep when the phone rang. It was Roger. "Dad's really sick," he said. "They don't think he's going to make it."

I literally flew to the hospital, where I found myself the last one to arrive. Why was that? The mind works in mysterious ways in times of crisis. Moments ago I was summoned out of a sound sleep by an emergency phone call. I jumped out of bed and worried about what would be the appropriate outfit to wear. At the hospital, I was concerned about whether or not I was the last one in the family to be called. I hugged Mom. "How is he?" I asked.

I remember hugging Mom long and hard, telling her that I loved her, asking how she was feeling, asking about you, and thinking, "God, I hope he doesn't die." Worse, I then thought, "And if he does die, I hope Mom doesn't."

"He's stable," she told me.

I saw you in the distance through a large window in the intensive-care unit. Doctors and nurses were huddled around your bed. Lots of people taking care of you. Still, the hospital smelled like death, but it was clean. The air was scented by the meticulous calculation of death. It smells inevitable.

VA hospitals are all the same, though. Remember the one in Reno? Maybe you should've checked out the Reno VA before you and Mom decided to retire there. That hospital was horrible. People would steal your stuff. They'd look for your change purse, then your shaver, and no one seemed to care. The nurses raised their eyebrows in a half-apology as if to say, "I'm sorry, but this isn't the Hilton."

You spent a lot of time in that Reno VA hospital. I used to take you for your cancer treatments. We'd slowly walk down to the basement to the Radiology Department. They'd put that silly robe on you. You looked so small in it. I couldn't recall you ever looking so tiny. You were always a strong, menacing big man. But there you were, inching down the hallway, a spindle of flesh and bone, walking in bare feet, your skinny legs showing and your butt exposed, making your war wound clearly visible.

"What would it be like to be shot?" I thought.

I was about to ask, when a nurse came in and escorted you to the room with a bigger gun than I'd ever seen. I followed along so they wouldn't hurt you. As soon as you put on those robes, I knew, no one respects you. Authority disappears. You become just another broken-down body in a building full of them. "My boy there, he's a comedian," you told the nurse. "He'll be famous someday." She smiled as if to say, "Yeah, right." Then she asked you to climb on a big, cold-looking metal table, and, by your reaction, it was cold.

This wasn't the picture of you that was stored in my mind.

You looked so helpless on the table, so alone. The nurse positioned the giant one-eyed monster above your scar. Then I was asked to step out. I heard her tell you, "Lay very still, Mr. Anderson." I could see you shaking slightly, and then I heard the machine come on. It sounded like a dentist's X-ray machine, or like a giant frozen-yogurt dispenser, but it lasted much longer.

Finally, though, that day's treatment was finished and you were allowed to leave. While you started changing clothes, I grilled the nurse about your condition and the intent of the treatment. "Well, it's radiation," she told me, "and it destroys the cancer cells. Or at least it slows them down."

I knew "slows them down" was closer to the truth. Anyway, you seemed relieved to get out of there. But we didn't make a clean getaway. "Mr. Anderson," another nurse called after us, "the social worker wants to see you about your benefits."

"Hmmm, social worker," I thought. "I'll handle this one."

Ready to do battle, I was pleasantly surprised by how nice this woman was. She was helpful and friendly. She talked briefly while you continued dressing, and you warmed right up to her, telling her that you had eleven children, that you were once a trumpet player, a veteran. She was seated in a chair next to where you were sitting on the bed. I was in a chair on the other side of the room.

"This is a tough one, this cancer," you told her after a brief coughing fit.

"You seem pretty tough yourself, Mr. Anderson," she said.

You smiled. In your heart, I think you already knew the outcome.

"I'll tell you something," you said to her, growing unusually mellow and reflective. "I know what tough is. My folks were alcoholics. When I was about ten years old, they took me and my sister to the little church in our town and put us up for adoption. Put us up before the congregation."

I was shocked. I'd never heard this before. I'd never once heard you speak about your childhood. For you, I thought, life began in the service. You were born in some barracks, wounded, and then you played trumpet with Hoagy Carmichael. My God! What was going on? And why weren't you telling me? Why were you opening up to this social worker, who, granted, was a nice woman, but a total stranger? I wanted to switch seats, turn you around, anything so that you'd be telling me. Instead, I just sat there, dumfounded and still, listening to you.

"I was adopted by this German family," you continued in a calm tone of voice that began to crack and waver as you went along. "Farmers. They didn't want another child. They already had children. They took me in as an extra hand. I slept in a different part of the house, ate different food at meals. You know, they'd offer their own kids seconds on dessert right in front of me and pass me right by."

Finally, you were crying. I could see the tears well up in your eyes and trickle slowly down your ruddy cheeks. I'd never seen you cry before. As you told the woman how you lied about your age to get into the service and escape your family, I desperately wanted to grab hold of you and hug you and ask why in the hell you'd never told me any of this.

Later, it struck me that we might've both been plagued by the same riddle of existence.

You blew your nose and apologized for crying, then wiped that big nose of yours.

"Did I tell you my boy is a comedian?" you asked her.

I guess you were proud of me, even though you didn't know how to tell me that yourself.

The social worker smiled. She looked at me, but I was in shock. I think she even asked me a few questions about comedy just to be polite.

"Gee, it must be exciting," she said.

I nodded. Back in Los Angeles, I was struggling to make rental payments on the tiny apartment where I lived in North Hollywood. It wasn't that exciting. But I could hardly think, let alone make conversation. I just wanted to put my arm around you and ask, "Why?" I suppose you might've wanted to ask your parents the same question.

But the moment passed without me saying anything.

While leaving the hospital, we walked up a flight of stairs. I remember being happy for the climb. I had to help you. It gave me a chance to slip my arm in yours, which pleased me, because what I really wanted and needed right then was to touch you, to tell you that I understood. I wanted to pat you on the back and say, "It'll be all right. Let's stop and get something to eat, and you can have all the dessert you want."

Signed,

Coffee cake for two
(in fact, make that the whole cake)

Dear Dad

I've been working hard editing my HBO special. Not that I'm vain or anything, but I've been bugging the director about my close-ups, asking him if we have enough. He told me that there are twice as many as usual.

"Well, I use my face to say a lot," I told him.

"Louie, I guarantee you it's enough."

The editor was in the background, nodding in agreement.

"Okay," I said, making a grumpy, little boy's face. "Let's see the drunk segment."

This segment was a departure for me. In a brief routine about drunks, I was actually playing a drunk. It was a big character piece, a chance for me to move away from my traditional stand-up act and on to a more serious side of comedy. That sounds funny, doesn't it? Serious side of comedy. But I think there is a serious side of comedy.

Portraying a drunk was easy for me. I had lots of time to study, thanks to you, Dad. I have all the moves down. That unfocused stare, wobbly knees, slurred speech, misdirected bursts of anger, repeating stupid phrases over and over until they go from being funny to plain stupid.

"Did you ever notice how hard it is to kick a drunk out of a bar?" I ask on the show. "It's impossible to lift them. And when you do manage to get them outside, they wake up just in time to push some bone-crushing bouncer in the gut and yell, 'Hey, watch it, or my friend Louie here will kick your ass.' You look at this killer, apologize, and explain that your friend is drunk, and usually they understand."

It was good that you finally quit drinking, Dad. I think you made everyone in the family happy with that choice. It was such a relief. But you started up again toward the end of your life.

I remember visiting you in Carson City. Mom, you and I went to Laughlin, or some small town, about two hours outside of Carson City. They had some kind of buffet Mom wanted to visit.

We sat there in the booth, Mom on one side, you next to her, and me opposite Mom. At this point, all the operations you'd had left you with only one-third of your stomach and not much of an appetite. An all-you-can-eat buffet like the one we were at had little appeal to you. But you liked to pull this trick. Mom would put her purse next to her and you would open it up, revealing a plastic baggy that you would fill up with chicken and buns, ribs, potatoes, and everything else that would fit. The only thing that didn't go in were the drinks.

I thought it was funny, and Mom was embarrassed. But she was too busy eating her mounds of food piled high on her plate. She loved to eat as much as I did. You'd laugh and joke about it. You were very sick then, walking with a cane, and a lot smaller and weaker in recent months. It seemed like you'd gone from the six-foot 225-pounder I knew as a kid to a frail five-foot-six-inch, 150-pound old man. I don't know what was more frightening to me: you getting drunk and violent or you getting old and feeble. The only reminder I had of you as the man I recognized from my childhood was the black beanie hat you wore when going out and your clip-on sunglasses.

After dinner we went out by the slot machines. You were leaning against one when a girl came around and asked if we wanted drinks. I ordered a 7-Up. Mom asked for water. And you ordered a beer. When I heard you order a beer, every emotion I'd forgotten since you quit drinking suddenly surfaced in a violent quake of nerves. I abruptly turned from the slot machine I was playing and looked at Mom. If Mom read the look in my eyes, she would've seen them say, "Oh God, please, not this again."

"Well," she said quietly, "he's really sick and he likes a beer once in a while. He doesn't act up or anything."

She was, I realized, a wonderful, understanding, smart, and, most of all, loving woman. She realized what I was realizing. That you were dying. I guessed a beer at that stage of your life couldn't hurt. If that's what kept you going.

On the way home, I sat closer to you than normal. That night I didn't sleep well. Neither did you. That week you went back into the hospital. It was a Tuesday. Mom and I visited you every day. You hated being there, but Mom wasn't able to care for you. At night she and I watched TV, unless I had some extra cash, and then I'd go down to the casino. On Friday I wandered down there and, after losing, wandered home, but before I opened the door, I knew something was wrong.

"Mom?" I called.

"In here," I heard her respond.

I walked through the little apartment to her room. She was tucking you into bed. "What's he doing here?" I thought. As sick as you were, you looked happy, like a little kid who got to stay home from school. Mom kissed you and then went into the living room.

"What's going on?" I asked.

"Well, there was a knock on the door and there was your father, along with a cab driver who wanted thirty dollars. He checked himself out. He told me he said they could stick their hospital up their butts."

"But he's too sick to stay home."

"What are you going to do?" Mom shrugged.

Late that night Mom woke me up.

"Would you mind helping your father?" she asked almost apologetically.

I remember helping you to the bathroom. I held you up, my arms around your chest. I couldn't believe how heavy you were, how helpless you were, how weak you seemed. How much longer would you be able to survive? In those brief moments, I started to think of our life together. There were a thousand and more things to say, but nothing seemed important enough. Just holding you up, I knew, was enough. It was all I ever wanted, all I ever needed to say. Touching you so closely, it was as if your life was being passed on to me, bonding, finally, and as I held you, I remember thinking, "I won't let you down, Dad. I won't let you down."

I returned you to bed, bent down, and placed a gentle kiss on your forehead. It felt warm, soft, and slightly damp. You woke up feeling tired. I was leaving that day, and I knew it would be the last time I would see you alive. I was right, too.

The next time I saw you was at the wake. I stood beside your casket, crying, and holding Lisa's hand. They put up a screen after the service, which lasted too long. The minister kept mispronouncing your name. He would say "Louie Armstrong" and, as usual, no one would say anything. Especially at a funeral. But after the fifth time, I spoke up and said, "Hey, it's 'Anderson.'"

This second-rate Baptist minister was my sister's ex-husband's minister. He spent a lot of time with you before you died. He went on and on about your being saved, and that you wanted the rest of us to be saved, too. After the service I pulled him aside and asked him not to go on too long at the grave site. I told him that you would've wanted it that way. He didn't question me.

I was still holding Lisa's hand and standing next to the casket when it came time to say goodbye to you. I pulled down hard on her hand and said, "Say goodbye to him, Lisa." She did, softly, and then I walked over to the casket, leaned over, and kissed you on the forehead. This time it wasn't warm, soft, and slightly damp. It was cold, hard, and very dry. At that moment I knew you weren't there.

They were about to close the casket when I asked for the ring you had on. It was the ring I'd given you for your birthday when I was ten years old. They stepped in front of us, removed the ring, then moved back and closed the lid. We all cried. With tears in our eyes, we moved back and readied ourselves for the job of carrying the casket. It was heavy, like the night I held you up. I wanted to put my arms around it and hold you once more, but I had my job.

Holding on to your casket, I walked down the chapel aisle,

noticing familiar faces red and moist from crying. Everyone was offering such loving, understanding looks. "If people were always like this," I remember thinking, "the world would actually be the happy, wonderful place it should be."

Signed,

I want to hold your hand

LA

Dear Dad

I've been waiting all day on pins and needles for a producer friend of mine named Sam to watch the videotape and give me his opinion. Talk about being nervous. After months, I've finally finished with the tape, fashioning it in a manner that will hopefully entertain an audience. I'm still planning on using it in my show at the Guthrie Theater in Minneapolis.

I've watched the damn thing so many times I feel like I've lived my life over several times. But I really think it's turned out good. I've added a few old snapshots and some 16mm home movies Roger sent me. So now the video opens with the family at the zoo, riding around on the merry-go-round. Then your music comes on over it. There's a picture of you taking a drink. All the interviews make up the middle. Then it ends with another photo of you looking straight ahead while all the kids tell what one thing they would say to you today given the chance. It ends with one of your songs and a lone, sad trumpet fading into quiet.

I met Sam about half an hour ago outside the editing facility where I've been working on the tape, ushered him into the tiny editing bay that's become my home away from home, and then shut the door and left him alone to watch. My fingers were crossed as I left, unable to watch him view. To kill time, I rummaged through the storage closet. I picked up several videotapes that were lying around, popped them into the machine, and watched a few minutes of each. Nothing very interesting, just some actors auditioning for parts and they didn't seem to be that good.

I'm still picking through this closet, even as I write this letter. Sam should be halfway through the video by now.

A moment ago, I finished watching a snippet from another horrendous video. This one was titled *The Pigs*, a title that intrigued me for obvious reasons. Was there another guy from Minnesota who made a video about his family? No. It turned out to be a punk-rock band, a really horrible punk-rock band. The piece was poorly recorded and badly shot. The person who shot it must've been related to the drummer, because all the close-ups were of him rather than the lead singer. I always wanted to be a rock star. I mean, who wouldn't?

Through a tiny window in the door, I then watched Sam watch the end of the videotape. There were the cutaways to each kid. "I love you," I heard Shanna say. "I love him and miss him. I wish I would have got to know him better. I miss him. I wish I would've been a better daughter. Thanks." Then came the music, your picture, and the tape was over.

I opened the door, turned on the light, and walked inside. "Well?" I said.

"Give me a minute or two," he said. "Let's get a bite to eat."

We walked outside together, Sam and I, heading for the East Indian Chicken restaurant. Neither one of us said a word, uttered a sound. My stomach was churning, nervous over what he would say. I kept trying to peek into his eyes, searching for some clue to his reaction.

However, Sam looked straight ahead and kept walking. He seemed to be lost in thought, and I figured that was good.

We turned into the little Indian deli, one of those California oddities. It was run by a Vietnamese family. Sam ordered pizza. I got a Chinese chicken salad. And we split a bottle of French mineral water. We faced each other over a tiny wooden table. I couldn't wait any longer.

"So what did you think?" I asked.

"It's great," he said matter-of-factly.

I nearly fell over. I looked hard into his eyes, like the police when they peered into mine, the eyes of the infamous Minnesota Snowmobile Fence. He liked it, great. But I knew Sam, and he'd surely have a criticism.

"It's too long," he said, "but it's good."

"Do you think I should play it at my show at the Guthrie?"

"Yes," he said without hesitation. "People there love you, and they should see all sides to you. They should laugh at your jokes and they should see the reverse of them. I don't know if it'll be funny, though."

It didn't matter. It wasn't supposed to be funny. It was a lot more than funny. I wanted to reach out and thank Sam, the first person who'd seen this tape outside of me and a technician at the editing place. It didn't seem right, though. Instead, I handed him a videotape and said, "When you get a chance, look at this. It's the film I really wanted to make."

Sam examined the tape.

"The Pigs?" he questioned after reading the title.

I smiled. The hard work, a labor of love, had already paid off. Still, the hard part, playing it in front of an audience, lay ahead. If I was going to continue to grow, it was a risk I had to take.

Signed,

The ex-pig

Dear Dad

Opening night at the Guthrie and a sold-out audience. I was really up for the show, jittery from nerves that reminded me of when I was starting out. The first half went well, but the second half is what worried me.

First I did a takeoff on Elvis. Don't ask me why. Maybe it was because I had the outfit. Then I left the stage to change back into Louie. The lights dimmed and the videotape started playing. In the dressing room, I quickly removed the Elvis costume and, with five minutes left on the tape, strained to hear the reaction from the crowd. I sensed people were restless. "Louie, come on!" I heard some of them shout.

"Oh shit," I thought, "there goes the review." A restless crowd, angry shouts. That's all the reviewer needed to make up his mind. Then the lights went up and I walked out to a decidedly mixed response. I attempted to explain why I showed the tape. I was worried. This wasn't a heckler I was battling, it was several thousand people reacting to a very intimate profile of my family. But when I looked out into the audience, I was able to see that some people had been crying. Good.

I ended the show with a few jokes, thanked everyone for coming, and then headed backstage to find someone who would be honest with me. Sue, the woman who booked me at the theater, was there.

"What did you think?" I asked.

"Well," she said, looking for the right words, "people were touched. We'll see tomorrow if we get any calls or complaints."

"The review will be shitty," I said.

"Who cares," she replied. "You're sold out."

That wasn't the point. I cared. I didn't perform to be sold out. I felt I had something to say. That's why I've always done it. You know that saying, Dad—if you touch one person, just one, that's enough. To me, that's bullshit. One is not enough, not nearly enough. I suppose it would be if everyone was trying to say something. But they aren't.

But, God, the thought of my first really bad review in my hometown sent me back to the hotel looking for a cheeseburger and fries.

Signed,

Gutsing it out with a Diet Coke and celery

Dear Dad

The review was bad, but I can't say that I didn't expect it. It hurt. But what really bothered me was that the reviewer didn't get it. He didn't understand where I was going. Nor did he try to understand. He wanted the old Louie Anderson. "Where were the fat jokes we love?" he wanted to know.

You know what I realized? People don't like you to change. They get comfortable with you and they want you to stay that way forever. They might change, but they don't want you to. It's scary. A good example is Richard Pryor. One of the great stand-up comics of all time, he quit drinking and doing drugs and suddenly people didn't think he was as funny.

I started out with an act consisting mostly of fat jokes. My first *Tonight* show was more than half fat jokes. The next time there were less, and less still the next and the next times. Finally, I decided to stop doing them. Why? For one, I was getting a lot of letters from fat people saying they didn't think I should do them. They felt the material was demeaning. Of course, I also got many complimentary letters from fat people. "I'm glad you can laugh at yourself," they'd say. "It helps me laugh at myself." But the reason I decided to say goodbye to fat jokes, the bread and butter of my routine, was that they just didn't feel good anymore.

It was a hard decision. People would ask, "Do you think

you'll still be funny?" That question amazed me. I have over two hours of comedy material, and at the very most I have fifteen minutes of fat jokes. Would I be funny if I wasn't fat? Was Pryor only funny when he drank and did drugs? No, I don't think so. Am I only funny when I tell fat jokes?

If I've learned anything through all this, it's that, in order to be happy with yourself, you must follow your heart. I bet you would have a few words to say about that, having forsaken your music career for kids and a bottle. See, you're the one who's making this journey. And if you can't travel with yourself, if you can't enjoy your own company, you have to figure out what's wrong and try to change.

My advice: screw the reviews and strive for the truest performance.

Signed,
Minnesota Slim
(at least I'm working on it)

Dear Dad

It's not that I like hotel living, believe me. I had planned to leave Minneapolis and return home a day or two after the Guthrie shows. But then I remembered that not long ago Rhea blurted out that you'd been married before. My suspicion was thus confirmed, and I'd meant to follow it up but never got around to it. Until earlier today.

I telephoned Mom and asked her about it, like I did months and months ago. Last time she didn't want to talk about it. This time I got a different response.

"Yes," she said quickly.

There was a short, awkward pause while the dust settled.

"Who was she?" I asked.

"A woman named Jesse," she said. "From Indiana. Your dad was married to her for two years. I never met her or heard anything about her, except that she was an alcoholic."

There was another pause while I digested the information.

"Were there any kids?"

"No."

There wasn't a lot more to say about this subject. Mom didn't seem to have anything to add. Nor did she seem like she wanted to. And I didn't know where to go with it.

A woman named Jesse. From Indiana.

I would've liked to have called her and asked what you were like and about the marriage, but I had no last name to go on. The shock probably would've killed her if she were still alive. So I chalked that off as a dead end. But then, without really having planned any of this, I picked up the telephone and dialed the county clerk's office in Detroit Lakes, Minnesota, the area where I've always thought you were from.

The woman who answered was pleasant and helpful, and I asked her if she could dig up your birth certificate and original residence. "Frazee Village," she informed me a few minutes later. "His mother's name was Ingeborg and his father's name was either Alfred or Albert. The handwriting is hard to read.

"His father, it seems, was a laborer, born in Sweden, and his mother was from Norway. They were forty-one and forty respectively on the date your father was born. August 12, 1901."

Listening to this woman recite this information put me into a trancelike state. I was barely able to mutter a thank you. To think that we lived together in the same house for twenty years and I never knew my grandparents' names or where you were born? Incredible. It was then that I decided to stay in Minnesota and finish this investigation by going back to the beginning. Your beginning.

Signed,

On the road again

Dear Dad

This morning started bright and early when I turned my Lincoln rental car onto Highway 55, heading toward Buffalo on my way to Detroit Lakes. I wanted to get some additional information on you and Frazee Village from the clerk's office in Becker County. Outside, the snow was blowing pretty hard, not helping the drive any. By pushing the button on the dashboard, I was able to get the temperature outside. It was seventeen degrees. It felt much colder than that.

I wasn't dressed for this type of weather. A long-sleeve shirt, a herringbone sports coat, and sneakers. Nor was I equipped with the proper snack food. Hungry, I pulled in to a place called Ron's Bait, Food, and Taxidermy. I glimpsed a sign advertising a free display of wildlife and fish, which sounded to me like a good laugh. Another sign on the door read "Taxidermy drop-off point."

Ron seemed to recognize me when I walked inside. I mentioned that I had an evangelist in the trunk that I wanted stuffed. He laughed.

"Don't stuff many evangelists these days," he joked.

I could see in his eyes that he was wondering what I was doing around these parts, two hundred miles north of the major cities. But he didn't ask. Instead, he asked for an autograph. I never know what to sign when people ask. Usually I write "Good luck" or "I hope you have a wonderful life." I always wonder what people do with my autograph once they have it. They probably end up crumpled on their dresser, alongside their watch and keys, later to be discarded, or they probably are forgotten in a pocket and go through the washing machine.

I handed Ron the signed piece of paper, and he handed me change for my two packs of gum and Diet Coke. Again, I couldn't help but notice Ron's puzzlement. My presence really threw him for a loop. He didn't hide his stare, didn't even try to. If he asked, I wondered, would I tell him the truth. "I am here to visit my father's birthplace," I would start. "I want to see the house where he first slept. The school where he first played hooky. The place where he smoked his first cigarette. The home from where the authorities removed him."

Having someone order you to leave your home must've been a horrible experience. Your parents, no matter how inhumane their treatment, are people no child wants to leave. Children only know Mommy and Daddy. "So what if they drink," I would imagine a child thinking. "So what if they beat me. Whose business is it if that goes on inside my home? I just want to figure out what I can do to make them love me."

I tried to imagine what you must've thought when they removed you: "Maybe if I was a better son they wouldn't drink. Maybe if I didn't eat so much. Maybe if I wasn't so in need of attention they wouldn't fight. When will I see my mom and dad again? What will happen to them? They aren't bad; it's me who's bad.

"Oh God, how can this happen to me. I'm only ten years old and I'm being taken away from the only place I know as home. Where am I going? What will they do without me?

"They depend on me. Who's going to pick them up after they've had too much to drink? Who's going to make sure they get into bed? Who will cut the wood to heat the stove, get the eggs, milk the cows? Who will make breakfast in the morning? My dad likes his eggs just so, and my mother likes her coffee with three and a half sugars and just a touch of cream. If you take me away, who will do these things?"

If Ron had asked, I might've had to let all that gush out. He would've thought I was crazy. It was better to simply sign an autograph. "I hope you have a wonderful life."

When our transaction was finished, I looked up at a pair of stuffed owl wings stretched out, claws wrapped around a post. Next to it was a deer, a rabbit, and next to the rabbit was an empty space. "A perfect spot for the evangelist in my trunk," I said.

Ron's Bait, Food, and Taxidermy, I noticed, also rented videotapes. There were two young guys scanning the shelves. One of them was on crutches. Probably a snowmobile accident, I decided. Maybe a deer ran out in front of him, hoping the guy would swerve, fall into the snow, and they could then deposit him at Ron's taxidermy drop-off. The two guys gave me that same what-are-you-doing-here look.

I was beginning to wonder that myself. But I kept repeating internally that I was on a mission, repeating it like a mantra. Ron's was beginning to give me the creeps. Especially that empty space next to the rabbit.

On the way out, I spotted a small animal mounted on the wall. I didn't know what species it was, but its eyes were more real than when it was alive, or so they seemed, and they were definitely looking right at me. "What are you doing here?'' they asked. For a moment they seemed to galvanize me in my tracks, stopping me like glue, but then I broke free and walked briskly to my car. "Just in time," I thought.

Maybe they were planning on stuffing me. A terrible thought. I would hate for people to come by, see me stuffed, and say, "Hey, he looks real."

Signed,

What am I doing here?

Dear Dad

I arrived at the Detroit Lakes Holiday Inn last night around nine-thirty, too tired to write to you, too tired to do anything except dial room service.

Mid-morning I strolled into the hotel lobby and got directions to the museum and county records center from the girl behind the desk. I could tell she wondered why I wanted to go there. I must've been the first person ever to ask.

"You go down 10," she said.

"Where's 10?" I thought.

". . . to around the Bonanza Steak House . . ."

That sounded familiar. Dad, did we eat there a few times? I vaguely remember it as a place where we got a ten-ounce steak, salad bar, and Texas toast. I remember that delicious Texas toast. We'd sit on backless benches and eat until we couldn't hold any more. And you'd always bring a baggy, which you'd fill with chicken from the salad bar.

". . . then you turn left, go two blocks, and turn right. You'll see an old church there. The cross is still up. And there's a red station wagon out front."

"Got it," I said. "Take 10, see the steak house, then the church and the red wagon."

"Bingo!" She smiled.

It didn't take me long on the highway before I saw the Bonanza Steak House. A few turns later I spotted the red station wagon, a Volvo. I didn't see a cross on what obviously used to be a church, but I did notice the word "museum" over the door. Remember when you worked at the museum in Carson City? Then, in your seventies, you worked as the janitor, cleaning up about four hours a day. Boy, you were tough. Never quit.

Inside, the small museum was a mess. The floor was all taped off in different sections, and there was a piece of scenery set against the wall. Close inspection told me that the history of Detroit Lakes was scheduled to be exhibited, though a thick layer of dust on the display seemed to indicate that no one was hurrying to set up. I walked over to the desk and looked around for someone to help me. There didn't seem to be anyone there. Taped onto a tiny silver bell on the counter was a sign that said "Ring for help." I rang.

Finally, a big blond girl greeted me. Like the girl who had given me directions at the hotel, this one also seemed bewildered by my presence as well as my inquiries into the past. They had newspapers dating back to 1901, she told me, and a few moments later she dropped several big, dusty old books of yellowed newspapers in front of me. I started to page through the delicate papers, noticing the stories and ads and realizing that in nearly a century things haven't changed that much. The top stories were about the government having too much control, crime, and the wedding of Mary McFadden to Harry Gunderson.

Under a section marked "Frazee Village," your birthplace, I hoped to find some mention of your arrival in this world. I read of numerous social functions. Betty Lindstrom's sister was visiting for two days. Early something-or-other from back east was in town. The Bensons' cow gave birth. Someone was advertising for a place to store a buggy. "Will trade sheep for space," his ad offered. I spotted an ad that seemed familiar. "Wanted: boy between 14 and 17 years of age to work after school and on Saturday. Only those willing to work need apply. H. H. Buckman Co."

You could've applied for this, Dad. Maybe you did. The paper was dated 1914. You would've been about thirteen, but you could've lied about your age. You did that a few years later to get into the service.

As I scanned the news of a century ago, the girl behind the desk told me that she was starting her break. "It's only nine A.M.," I thought. "What time did you come to work, six?" She was going on a break when there were still lots of papers to go through. Oh well. I continued going through the papers, until I heard giggles. The coffee break was over.

"Did you find anything?" the girl asked.

"I'm looking, but no luck," I said. "Not much about Frazee here."

"We have the Frazee papers if you want them," she said.

Her revelation was exciting.

"Why didn't you tell me sooner that you had them?" I asked.

"You didn't ask," she said.

Half an hour later, I knew who in Frazee had gotten married, had children, been robbed and elected, but I didn't find anything about your first day on the planet or your family. Too bad.

Signed,

Not giving up

Dear Dad

Okay, okay. As if I was drawn by a giant magnet, I finally pulled into Frazee Village, a big farm town with low white buildings and steam rising from smokestacks. Driving in, I wondered what they raised on the farms. Chickens, maybe? No, it had to be something bigger. Then I passed a giant turkey on the corner of the hill. "Tommy," I yelled out. "Tommy the turkey." That's what I said in honor of my little brother.

Turkey town. What did the population sign say? I would've seen it had that humongous turkey not caught my attention. I drove slowly, taking in the sights and the fragrance of the small settlement, scouting the layout. The place looked like something Norman Rockwell would've painted. Pure Americana. A few buildings made up the center of the town. When you were born, though, the town was called a village. Maybe your stories about dirt floors, no windows, and wooden wheels are true.

Even though it was cold and blowing, people were out walking the streets. They were moving with a sense of purpose. It was around noon, so they were probably on their way to lunch. Perhaps some were taking a break from work to go home and visit their mates, steal an afternoon hug and kiss. There was a little church sitting alone atop a hill. As I passed, I wondered if you'd ever set foot inside. Did you pray that your parents would stop drinking, stop hurting themselves, stop making you feel bad? Did you pray to get the hell out of there?

I drove by a small wood-frame farmhouse where you could've grown up. It looked old enough. It looked like the barn rafters would be full of stories and whispers from another era. Eventually, I turned down an unsigned street, circled around, and found myself on Main Street, where I noticed a gentleman walking across the street. I pulled up alongside and rolled down my window.

"Hey, excuse me," I called. "Where's a good place to eat here?"

He paused for a moment, reflecting before giving me an answer, and then he pointed out two locations. One on the other side of the street and one right in front of the car.

"Which one is better?" I asked.

He shrugged his shoulders. In his eyes I saw that small-town life had taught him that he shouldn't take sides. I almost asked him who he voted for in the presidential race. But it seemed clear that he had nothing to say on any issue, particularly where I should eat lunch. I thanked him and he went on his way.

I picked the café closest to me. It had community seating, where everyone sat with whoever else happened to be there. I hadn't seen that forever. But there they all knew each other anyway. I picked an empty table with five chairs and scanned the joint. Behind me was the window where the waitresses yelled their orders to the cook. A woman with a beehive hairdo and black stretch pants that were too tight for her ample figure rushed around serving people their food. A woman about Mom's age sat alone at a double table against the wall, nibbling toast and working a crossword puzzle.

The specials were written on a chalkboard. Chicken and dumpling soup and sandwich, $2.50; shrimp platter special, $3.50.

"What'll ya have, hon?" the waitress asked.

"How's the soup?"

"Good."

I ordered the soup, and as my ice water arrived a man who I guessed to be in his late sixties, early seventies sat at the end of my table. For a moment I expected him to say something like, "Hi, Louie, your dad sent me. He's outside, waiting. He wants to know if he should come in and join you." I was ready to respond, to tell him to bring you in, but when he spoke, it was only to order the shrimp platter.

To make conversation, I asked him the age of the town, though what I really wanted to know is if he knew of you or your parents. He said the town was about a hundred years old.

"The turkey business has always been big here," he explained. "There's an old plant down the street, but since that closed down . . ."

His voice trailed off as he finished the sentence and seemed to drift to another place. I was set to ask him another history question when he returned.

"The town used to be one mile west of here." He nodded as if letting me in on a local secret. "They moved the center of town."

Oh no. Was I in the wrong place?

"How long ago did they move it?" I asked.

"Not sure," he said, rubbing his chin.

"Was it here in 1901?"

"Oh yeah."

I was relieved. This was the right place. I explained to him that my father was born in Frazee and that I'd come to examine his roots.

"What was your dad's name?" he asked.

"Anderson. Louie Anderson."

"Might as well be Smith," he laughed. "Lots of Andersons up here."

My soup arrived separate from my Tommy-the-turkey sandwich on dry wheat toast. "That'll be right up," the waitress chimed. The old man's shrimp platter came, too. The shrimp looked small, not much of a meal, but I guessed the guy was probably sick of turkey. The soup was great. I slurped it down quickly. Maybe you once sat here and slurped your soup? Oh, that's right. They didn't have soup then.

For several moments we ate in silence. Then, just as I was about to ask the old guy more questions, a big Swede walked in and asked the man if he could sit down. "I spoze," he said. The way he said it wasn't very encouraging, and it made me feel as if I'd lost contact with your past. I was suddenly the outsider. However, listening to their conversation, I learned the Swede had cancer, that he'd recently had an operation on his prostate. He looked at me when he said it, as if I shouldn't have been eavesdropping and should mind my own business. Then he gave the old man a look that said he should stop discussing it.

Eventually, I let go of their talk and finished my soup as my sandwich was set down. They'd made it on white bread and spread a thick layer of mayonnaise. I was going to send it back, but when I looked at the girl stationed at the register, she looked awfully similar to the girl at the hotel and the girl at the museum. So, like the others, I let it go, nodded a goodbye to the old man, and paid my bill.

I walked across the street to the offices of the newspaper, an eight-page, fact-filled tabloid covering Frazee. The major stories in that day's edition were anticipating 1991, the town's centennial, and a shortage of ideas on how to celebrate Turkey Day. In other news, the local pastor urged parents to bring their children to Sunday school; a letter to the editor requested the new veterans' home not be built beside a garbage dump. "Veterans have suffered enough," the writer maintained. There was a recipe for a peaches-and-cream dessert. And fun facts informing readers that centipedes had only twenty-one to thirty legs and not hundreds of legs as most people think, and that Lindbergh was the first person to cross the Atlantic alone, but the ninety-second to simply cross it.

For a measly eight pages, the newspaper sure provided a lot of information, not to mention pictures. My favorite was the Future Farmers of America photo. As always, there was a fat kid in the center of it, posing with his prize-winning hog. For some reason, I know their motto: "Learning to do, doing to learn, learning to live, living to serve." I wonder if there's a dirty version to that?

Ahh. As I turned the pages, I came across the really important stuff: the school lunch menu. Why wasn't this on the front page? Monday was sausage pizza, peanut butter or butter sandwich, green beans, fruit sundae, two percent whole milk. There was a cancer-rich meal. Tuesday was overfried chicken. Wednesday was cheeseburgers. On

Thursday spaghetti with cheese sauce was being served, and Friday was tuna subs. I read that and thought, "Skip school Thursday and Friday."

Oh, too bad. Clara someone died. It was on top of the obituary column. Obituaries are always weird to read. Weird yet morbidly fascinating the way everyone is summarized and then listed in neat rows just like they're buried at cemeteries. I still have your obituary, Dad, the one I clipped out of the newspaper. It was a long one, listing all of us. When you died, there was no listing in the Frazee paper. You'd left at such a young age there was probably no one around who even remembered you. Doesn't matter. I'm glad you left. Frazee's a nice place to visit, but I wouldn't want to die there.

On my way back to Minneapolis, I glanced at Frazee's population sign and had the strange feeling that, as I passed, it went down a notch. I felt the eyes on that big turkey statue watching me leave. I was glad to be leaving. Though I hadn't found any physical trace of your early life, I suppose I really hadn't expected to. I just wanted to be there for a little while, to just sit among the villagers, slurp my soup and dream.

Signed,

Leaving Frazee
(on a wing and a drumstick)

Dear Dad

For me, the day March 3, 1989, began at 8:20 A.M. It had been snowing heavily all night in Minneapolis. My friend Jim was set to pick me up at 9:30 to help me on this final leg of the journey. I laid in bed for a while, switching TV channels and stopping on one which had a talk show whose guests were the guys from the *Little Rascals* show. Spanky McFarland was the only recognizable one. The others bore no resemblance to themselves as kids.

However, they still all sounded like they did when they were young. I guess we all have this immutable essence to our character, like a fingerprint, that stays the same throughout life and makes us what we are. If that's true, age, I figure, is nothing to fear, except that it means we're getting closer to the end.

I was eating my healthy breakfast of bran muffins and coffee when Jim finally arrived, a little late. He blamed it on the weather and described how it had taken him an hour to travel ten miles. He also said it was supposed to snow another six to nine inches, in addition to the five we'd already had.

"I don't think you'll get out of here tomorrow," he said.

Sometimes I feel as if I've never left, that my career, where I live, everything that's happened to me is a dream, a mirage of sleep. As Jim gave me the weather rundown, I was in one of those moods. Maybe I was buried in a deep freeze, I thought, stuck way deep in a snowdrift, and when it all finally thaws, I'll wake up and find myself back home with you and Mom and the rest of my brothers and sisters.

"Maybe we should go now," I said.

"Maybe not," he replied.

"I think if I don't go today I'll never go," I said, biting into a bran muffin.

I decided to call first.

"Fort Snelling Cemetery," the girl answered.

"I'd like to find out where my father's buried," I said.

"You would like the location of a grave?"

No, I wanted to say, I would like to find out where my dad is buried. But maybe, I thought, she handled every question with a response that was practiced, memorized, and lifted from the instruction manual, in order to keep a safe distance from people's emotions. I gave her your name, Louie W. Anderson, and waited while she checked.

"There are two of them," she said. "What's your mother's name?"

"Ora."

"Okay. He's in Section W, Plot 4446. When you get here, come to the first building on the left."

I hung up and started getting dressed. Jim and I decided we'd head in that direction and, if the weather proved too severe, we'd turn back. I put on my warmest California clothes, but realized it wasn't going to be enough for the cold. And I brought along my tape deck, earphones, your favorite beanie hat and eyeglasses, and pictures of you that Mom sent me. I had some things to share with you.

As we drove, the snow swirled around like we were in *The Wizard of Oz*. It was really bad outside. We passed a couple of cars stuck in the ditch. The Highway Patrol helping them, a relief to me. I didn't want to have to stop and help, but sometimes you don't have a choice. It struck me as a day when only cops, insurance agents, tow trucks, and moms and dads would be on the road.

To me, the snow looked beautiful. Big flakes blowing in a million different directions. I imagined us in a giant glass snow scene that had been shaken hard and set on someone's desk to admire.

Finally, we saw a sign. National Cemetery, one and one quarter miles.

It seemed like I was standing still while little cars whipped by me on their way home. I had to roll down my window to see the side of the road. The snow had worsened and the visibility was down to nothing. With the window down, I heard gunshots, and immediately knew someone was being buried. I heard the second round.

"Did you hear that?" I asked Jim.

"No."

The firing ceased, and I imagined people hurrying back to their cars to escape the cold and the wind, trying to prevent their tears from freezing to their face.

We passed through the large, iron gates of Fort Snelling National Cemetery, driving up the long entrance blanketed by soft white powder. No one had driven on the snow yet, I noticed. Rounding the first building on the left, I pulled the car up to another building that looked as if they held services inside, and parked in the only open space, one marked "Rifle Squad." I realized then that I was at the wrong building.

I backed up and returned to the first building, got out, and ran up the snow-covered walk, passing a flagpole whose flag was flying at half-mast. I wondered who died. Then I realized it must always be that way. As I approached the building, I remembered that I had forgotten the paper on which I'd written your plot's location. I was so preoccupied with other thoughts. Like why was I doing this? Like remembering the time I drove Jim to his father's grave so he could read him some letters.

I opened the heavy wood door and walked inside. A girl at the desk asked if I needed help, and I told her that I'd forgotten the paper. She didn't respond, but automatically pulled out this sheet of paper that looked like a big seating chart to a concert hall. It was a layout of the cemetery. She asked for the name.

"My dad's name is Louie W. Anderson," I said, though before I finished, she was gone, and before I noticed that she'd returned, she was explaining where the grave was located. I asked her to show me, and as she pointed out the window, a white hearse pulled around the corner.

"You have funerals today?" I asked.

"Eleven of them," she said.

I suppose death doesn't care what the weather's like.

"The numbers are on the back of the tombstones," she told me. "You go to row 4426 and walk in twenty graves and you'll be at 4446."

Thanking her, I turned to go back to the car and felt my mind grappling with the big question of why I'd come to visit my father's gravesite. Without following a preconceived plan, I'd been mysteriously drawn here, it seemed, by some inner compass, led here by a powerful force of emotions that was suddenly building to a peak.

I climbed back into the car, then decided to take a piss before Jim and I traveled out there. I drove back to the building where the Rifle Squad van was parked. Inside, there was a set of keys hanging on a door. I wanted to take them out and give them to the proper person, but decided to forget about it. Let someone else be responsible for a change.

When I got back to the car, it had, believe it or not, gotten colder. The snow was blowing harder and harder. I pulled the car onto the long driveway, the one you've seen in every cemetery scene in the movies. I figured your row must've been about halfway up, but the road was divided into two one-way sides, so I went up one lane and then down the other. Since there was no place to turn around, I had to go all the way to the end, a cul-de-sac.

As I approached, I saw in the distance a green tent set up that was similar to the one Mom sat in as they lowered your casket into the ground. At that point, servicemen relieved us of our flag duty and folded it into a three-cornered George Washington hat, and handed it to her. Instead of reaching out and hugging them, Mom smiled and accepted the flag, putting it into her lap and returning her sad eyes downward. But the tent I saw this time was empty. The people either had left or hadn't yet arrived. The snow made it impossible to tell.

We made the turn, and stopped a ways down, but still couldn't make out the numbers.

"Should I get out and see?" Jim asked.

"No, I'll do it," I said.

The number was 5626. Too far up. I drove down further. As I started to get out, holding my little bundle, Jim stopped me.

"Better take my boots," he urged.

"No," I said, but then I realized that I might be a while and I didn't want to lose any toes. As I kicked off my Nikes, Jim teased me about having a lot of money but no boots. I was going to make a joke, but Jim's teasing, I knew, was only him expressing concern, wishing I'd be more responsible for my well-being. I put on the boots, grabbed my stuff, and headed out to the row in front of the car.

Number 3426, I saw. Damnit, I overshot by ten rows. Dad, even though you're dead, you weren't making it easy on me. I couldn't believe how deep the snow was, and yet, all around, the marble headstones were perfectly clear. As I trudged past the stones, I noticed the names: Smith, Johnson, Pepperdine, Lewis, Phillips. God, the wind was fierce. I put my headphones on; they're big and they warmed my ears. My hands were stuffed in my pockets as deep as I could push them in.

Finally, I came upon number 4426. Your row.

I turned down the row, thinking: "Only twenty graves down. Count them." I felt the urge to cry, but held back. "Thank God for the boots," I thought. I looked at the names of your neighbors: Bowman, Walsh . . . With each name, I imagined how many other children could be walking with me. Then I saw the graves of spouses. "Mary, wife of . . ." I wondered if Mom wants to be buried here?

Twenty stones in I saw the name William and wondered if they hadn't made a mistake. Then I kicked away some snow and saw the entire name:

Louie William Anderson.
Born August 12, 1901—Died April 9, 1980.
World War I. Bugler.

From my little sack, I removed the black corduroy cap you wore, the one I remember you in, and placed it on the edge of the gravestone. I plugged the other set of the headphones I'd brought into the tape machine and draped them on each side of the headstone. Earlier, I had read each of these letters into a tape recorder. I wanted you to hear them and turned on the tape player. I felt we should listen to them together.

With my voice reciting in the background, I removed the glasses you wore, noticing how worn and well used they were and how large your head must've been. They slipped onto my head easily. How many times I remember those glasses sitting on the edge of your nose, your middle finger on the right hand pushing them up so you could read your Webster's. Your eyes weren't so bad. Looking through them, I could see pretty clearly.

Looking through your eyes, the world didn't seem that bad. What did you see, I wondered, that I didn't?

I knew the answer. After all this, I knew.

It wasn't the same with me, I realized. Even through your eyes, I saw the world as a brighter, happier place. And I was happy for that.

A few moments ago I gazed out over the endless rows of headstones. They seemed to form the letter W. Is that why they called this Section W? I listened to a few more of the letters being read, then reached into my pocket and pulled out a white envelope Mom had given me. It was filled with pictures of us and a note from her that said, "Dear Louie, I hope that these are okay. I hope the trip was a good one. Love, Mother."

The first photo was of you and Mom, taken a long, long time ago, probably when you still called her "my darling Toy." In the next you two are sitting in a booth at a restaurant. You have on a tuxedo and look handsome. Was this before a performance? Another photo shows all of us in South Dakota. I'm standing next to you. I must've been about five years old. You have a cigarette in one hand, your glasses—the ones I was wearing—are on, and I have a baseball cap on, just as I do now.

Right now the tape is continuing on about your career, but there're more pictures to sort through. Here's one of you clowning around. Tears are starting to form in my eyes. I can't help it anymore. I'm crying, I'm writing, I'm looking at photographs. In this next picture, you're older and sicker, holding a can of beer and smiling. The tape continues to play but I can't hear it, and finally it stops. The letters are over and now it's just you and me, sitting out here in the blizzard.

"Here's a photo of you rolling a Bull Durham. God, I can almost smell the tobacco. You're smiling in the picture, and I know right now, at this moment, you're here with me. I'm crying hard and loud. I'm not holding anything back. I realize how much I miss you, you bastard. This last picture is a close-up of you. There is a cigarette in your mouth, and you're wearing the same hat and glasses that I have on now. I see the look on your face, in your eyes, and you're looking directly at me, and I hear you say, "I love you, Louie."

I know, Dad.

I forgive you. I understand.

I realize why I have come here and what I've been looking for all this time. I wanted to be with you. And now I am and always will be.

Oh yeah. There's one more thing that I haven't said but want to. And that one thing is, I love you.

Your son,

Louie

Dear Louise

Through a peculiar set of circumstances our paths have crossed and I feel compelled to write and share my experience with you.

I was browsing in a bookstore last week when I came across your book. Without knowing what it was about and being totally unfamiliar with you (your face or your work), I purchased the book. I suppose I was just meant to read it.

I too am an adult child of an alcoholic father. Until very recently I could never have said that to anyone. I built a fantasy world for myself which carried over into my adult life, long after the death of my father. So many experiences in our lives are similar—if not identical. Your book was wonderfully therapeutic for me. Thank you!

However, that is not the only reason for this letter.

I began reading your book at home and finished it on a plane ride to Minneapolis on Friday. There I sat (seat belt securely fastened), crying over the last chapter. Immediately after checking into the hotel, I walked across the road to the cemetery at Fort Snelling and visited your dad. I hope you don't mind; I felt very close to you and your family after reading your book and there I was, across the street, just feet away from your father's grave. Somehow it's what I needed to do at that time.

Forgive me for intruding, but you shared some intimate family secrets, so I didn't think you'd mind.

I loved your book and if I can ever stay up late enough to watch you on television, I know I will love your humor.

Warmly,

A Bookstore Browser

Dear Mr. Anderson

I was so touched by the excerpt of your book I saw in the TV Guide, I just had to write to you. It seems we have had similar families, and I too have thought of writing to my father. I haven't yet.

There is no doubt that drinking parents affect all family members. I hope you realize, it was not you to blame for his actions. After all, he was the adult. You ask why adults who drink do the things they do? I don't think they know themselves. Alcohol makes people change and do things they normally wouldn't do.

Please don't carry this blame throughout your life. I can assure you, you were not at fault.

Now that you are an adult, reflecting on the love you missed growing up, and lack of security, don't torment yourself. The past is gone and can't be changed. Live for today.

I hope I am able to help fill the emotional void you carry just a little with this letter.

And I think I can answer the biggest mystery of your life, if you allow me. Yes. Your father did love you. I know he did, as well as I know my father loved me, yet he never said so. My father too died of cancer twenty-five years ago. He never told me anything at all about his childhood, and I thought that odd. People from that generation were different. Their lives were different. The world also was different.

I'm now the same age my father was when he died. I see

life so differently than I did twenty-five years ago. With age comes wisdom, and in time you will know these things I speak of with certainty.

I want to thank you for sharing this personal part of your life. It has helped me and I'm sure many others who have had a similar past.

I also wish to add, my wife and I love you just as you are.

Very sincerely,

Older and wiser

Dear Louie

I bought your book Wednesday night at my church book-store, and read it Wednesday night and Thursday during the day at work until I finished it. It's great.

I, too, am a fat ACOA. My father is still alive and still drinking. I'm two months younger than you, and I too was a hippie, and hated gym glass. I became an entertainer also . . . and crave the applause the way you describe.

I have been going to ACOA meetings for almost four years, and am now clean from drugs with help from Narcotics Anonymous.

Your life and mine have taken different paths, but the feelings you describe are the same as mine. I am tempted to send the book to my father. Maybe I will.

Thanks,
David

Dear Louie

I grew up near you, Louie, and when I heard your comedy I felt like I was listening to my big brother. . . . I just finished reading *Dear Dad* straight through and I had to write and thank you. My family was living a similar story not too many blocks from you. But the addict was my mom and her drugs of choice were religion and medically prescribed pills.

I grew up in St. Paul, on York Avenue. If you follow the tracks, it's only thirteen minutes from the projects where you and my friend Abby lived. She used to trade sandwiches with me at school. Her mom made homemade bread. She preferred Wonder Bread. Her mom's bread was cut two inches thick; you could hardly get your mouth around the sandwich.

My sister and I went to Ames for kindergarten. We had Mrs. Iffey. Did you? My sister fell off the jungle gym and her two front teeth went through her lower lip and she still has a white scar. Then we were transferred to Blessed Sacrament. When I wore my navy uniform and knee socks my thighs rubbed together and made a rash. Too much divinity sale candy I guess. Did you ever play in "Swede Hollow" or on the "Big Sandy" Hill, and come home with burrs stuck to your socks? Did you have socks?

Like your family, my family pretended Mom was normal. I was the one who had to figure it out or I might go to bed again and never get up, like she did. That was the wonderful thing about *Dear Dad* for me. The same years you were trying to figure out what happened to make your dad do what he did, I was doing the same thing with my ma. It took me over twenty years to do it, too.

I inherited the religion drug, but after a rape by a guy with a razor knife I became really guilt-ridden and tried to kill myself and survived a fatal overdose. My mom had taught me it was better to be murdered than lose your virginity. Anyway, food was one of my comforts, but after the rape, sex became my drug of choice.

I found out very late, much the way you did about your dad's family, that my mom had been a nun for seven years before she married Dad. The guilt and shame of leaving her order destroyed her and nearly destroyed me. I wrote a book about these things and it has finally allowed me to complete my grieving.

The truth allowed me to forgive my mom, my dad, and God. Finally, it doesn't matter if anyone ever validates my search; Louie Anderson knows how you just gotta find out.

I'm just starting to remember the joy of my childhood, the parts I can cherish. *Dear Dad* has given me comfort and healing and joy—we can finally be separate from the suffering. I love it and I love you more than ever for writing *Dear Dad*.

Love,

A graduate of Ames Kindergarten

Dear Louie

I'm thirty years old and this is the first letter I've ever written to a celebrity but I was so moved by your book that I had to write. I've read it a couple of times, partly to try to figure out what made your father the way he was but mostly because I found you very easy to relate to. You see, I too am overweight and know the rejection, discrimination, and loneliness that come along with it. A couple of years ago I lost eighty-two pounds on the Weight Watchers diet only to put about forty of it back on. Food seems to be my vice when I'm nervous, upset, or sad. I keep working at it. I can only speak from a woman's point of view but when you're fat that's all most people seem to see. They can't get past it. It doesn't matter that you might be a nice person, one who has a lot to offer as a friend. Most guys don't like chubby or fat women. You can dress nice, have a nice personality and a good sense of humor but they never get to find that out because they have visions of a size eight. So you starve yourself all day only to give in to a Snickers bar at night.

I've been thinking about your father, Louie, and I really think he loved you and still does wherever he may be, but he was just too wrapped up in his own life and pain to show it. The way I see it, the loss is a lot more his than yours. He missed out on getting to know his children. He never knew his son Louie, a sensitive, loving, caring son who any father would be proud of. You're looking for answers, Louie, but there might not be any. All you can do is learn from your father's mistakes and do things differently with your kids. Don't let their legacy be a cold, snowy cemetery, a pair of glasses and a hat. Be active in their lives. Hug and kiss them.

I hope writing this book has helped you, Louie, but after you get done hashing all this over, put it behind you and look to your future or it will eat away at you like a cancer. I can see your pain right through the pages. Life will get better. Don't turn your back on God. Pray for some inner peace and happiness. Eventually it will come. God bless.

A friend in Massachussetts

P.S. Stop the fat jokes, Louie, not because I find them offensive but because you're too nice a guy to have to let people have a laugh at your expense. There's a big difference between laughing with you and laughing at you. Besides, you're very funny without the fat jokes.

Dear Mr. Anderson

I wanted to write and thank you for opening your life and writing your book. I can relate to most of your pain, not because my father is an alcoholic but because he left us when I was seven years old. I am now twenty-four and married and I still remember taking him his shaving kit—he drove a truck for a living—and watching him drive out of my mom's and the eight of us kids' lives.

For three years my mom supported us by working three jobs and still taking classes at the local college to better herself. We were on welfare, too. I remember the food baskets and toys we got on holidays. When the local child development center was getting ready to take six of us from my mom, she took us instead to a semi-orphanage where she could stay and see we got raised right, and we stayed together.

I always was very angry with my father as I grew up but later those feelings just numbed. I learned that I had to forgive my father for my own good but still had no desire to see him, even when he made arrangements to see the rest of the family.

Since reading your book, I wanted to write him and ask questions I could never answer. Why did you leave? Don't you love me? And so many others.

Thank you, Mr. Anderson, for restoring the feelings and

good memories of my father. If you ever make it out our way, I will be in your audience.

Thanks a lot,

A deserted daughter

Hi Louie

(I hope when I send this it gets to you.)

Thank you very much for writing your book *Dear Dad*. Even though a lot of it differed from my circumstances, a lot was the same.

I am an adult child of two alcoholic parents. I never knew this until after I was married (and yes, I married an alcoholic who is now recovering). My mother is recovering, too (or so she always leads me to believe anyway, but sometimes I doubt it), and my dad is very much in denial. My husband has had one relapse in a year.

I really want to tell you about the relapse. It's the kind of morbid-funny humor you might like. I came home from work to find my husband almost drunk and having a mild Antabuse reaction. (Antabuse is a drug they sometimes use to help alcoholics stay sober; it makes you sick if you drink while you're using it.) Actually it was more of a moderate reaction. He was bright red, but still breathing. Anyway, I grabbed my baby, packed, and headed to a phone where I called my parents to tell them all. When I got to their house (they told me to come stay with them), I went to their refrigerator, found a glass of something, and took a big swig of . . . VODKA LEMONADE! Either Mom or Dad had been on the phone with their hysterical daughter with drink in hand! I couldn't believe it. I felt like I had nowhere to go and nobody but a bunch of damn drunks to turn to.

Another thing about your book that was ringing close to home was the weight. Although I am not really overweight, I am bulimic and have been so for almost eight years. I've been in treatment and everything—it's all really laughable! I do okay now but have my moments. The big thing that I am not getting over is the guilt and self-esteem thing. I can't think of myself as worthwhile although I'm ready to. I have had enough of this life.

By the way, I'm twenty-one, have a baby son, and sell shoes at Sears. If you're ever in the neighborhood and need some new shoes, come visit me at the mall.

Sincerely,

A shoe salesperson

Dear Louie

It's 4:30 A.M. and I have just stayed up all night reading your book. I'm writing because I want you to know how deeply you have touched me . . .

I stopped watching your routines quite some time ago for two reasons. The first is that as a fat adult child of an abusive family, your jokes just hurt me too much. I felt as though you didn't understand—that you didn't get it. There was such shame and desperation and pain in my very soul and your comments took what was the most fragile and vulnerable part of me and made fun of it. Being humiliated in this way was an all-too-familiar experience for me. The second reason I stopped following your work was that it was quite painful watching you hurt yourself through your routine. You see, I knew what it was all about—where it had to be coming from. When we're raised in an abusive and unloving family environment, we grow into adults who treat ourselves in abusive and unloving ways. And so I couldn't expose myself to the feeling of being hurt by you or watch you abuse yourself. My heart goes out to both of us.

And mine is not the only heart you've touched. It was a patient of mine who gave me your book (I'm a therapist). He has dissociated from many childhood events and feelings and your book is helping him put the pieces of himself and his life together. And so I also am grateful for this resource that is aiding me in helping this dear man heal his wounds.

I wish for us, and for all the walking wounded, that our search brings us to a better life—a life filled with true happiness, inner peace, and love. I am so glad for you for the personal journey which you have undertaken and, I assume, continue to be on. I am on such a journey in my life as well. And I thank you for helping me with my growth by sharing some of your own.

The next time I'm aware of one of your appearances, I will be watching with joy and enthusiasm. I'm glad for having had the chance to get to know you a little bit. The people whose lives are entwined with yours are indeed fortunate.

Louie, I truly hope you have a wonderful life—these are your words, but please know that the sincerity and sentiment with which they're spoken come deep from my heart.

With love,

A therapist

(I really hope this reaches you, Mr. Anderson.)

Dear Louie Anderson

I just finished your book and I must say that that took so much courage to tell the world about your life and what you went through. Like many many people in this world, I am also an adult child of an alcoholic. I can relate to your story— I understand. And yes, it made me cry. It was so emotional and so powerful because (and I hope this doesn't bore you as I'm sure you get many letters a day from people telling you their stories now but it's always nice to talk to someone who understands) . . . my mom and dad are recovering alcoholics. My dad was admitted to a hospital two years ago for treatment of his alcoholism but unfortunately both Mom and Dad still carry their symptoms even though they don't drink anymore. The only thing I remember from his treatment—my brother, sister, and I weren't asked to attend a treatment session—was that his last assignment was to write a letter and go to his father's grave and read it. I believe he wrote the letter but he never went to the grave and when you ended your story with you at your dad's grave, I cried. If my dad were able to talk to his dad, I know it would make a big difference, but it does take time. I'm going to give him your book. I'm not sure he'll take it—because he's not too healthy yet but what have I got to lose? If only he knew what it was like on the other side. I am so glad I have chosen to go through recovery in my life. It's probably the best thing I could ever do for the children I plan to have in the future.

I always dream that someday I'll be able to let kids and teenagers know that there's hope. And I think that your way of helping by writing and sharing your life with me and the rest of the world was a brave and wonderful way to get through to people.

Take care of yourself,

Another adult child

Dear Louie

   I just bought your book for my sixteen-year-old son Joey.
I have this deep aching feeling in my stomach that my son,
who has a verbally abusive father, may be so depressed he
would consider suicide. I divorced Joey's father six years ago
because he was lazy and selfish and never took the respon-
sibility to care for his children or myself. I worked two jobs
but I finally had to give up on the marriage. I am now
remarried to a wonderful man and live in New England.
Joey and his brothers chose to stay in Seattle with their father
when I remarried rather than move from their friends and
school and I feel totally helpless.
   Joey is over six feet tall and about 300 pounds. He is so
sensitive and easygoing and is well-liked but shy. His father
changed a lot after the divorce. I feel he is taking it out on
Joey for my leaving. Joey's brothers are okay in my husband's book because they do well in school and are popular
and will talk back to him if he's out of line. But with Joey
he constantly calls him names about being fat and calls him
stupid for getting bad grades and takes all personal things
Joey likes away from him. I have tried talking to Joey and
tried to get him to come live with me but he says he can
stick out one more year until he graduates. I hope so, Louie.
Joey says he won't even try asking girls out anymore because
he knows the answer. He wants to drive but his father is
always punishing him and saying he can't drive for this

reason or that. Joey says he wants to lose weight but has no will power, and his dad won't get special food for him just because he's on a diet.

I'm hoping Joey will be enlightened by your book. He loves you, Louie. He can recite every special you've done by heart. I hope your book hits home with him where I have tried but failed. I love my son, Louie. I just wanted to write to you and thank you for sharing and letting Joey know he's not alone. He and his brothers are spending Christmas with us this year and I'm counting the days.

I hope your book is the turning point in Joey's life because you are someone he admires and I know it will be his favorite gift from his mom.

Thanks for allowing me to share my feelings with you. Your book made me feel better and I hope you accomplish all that you want to in life. God bless and keep making people happy by just being yourself.

A grateful mother

Dear Mr. Anderson

I have never written to a celebrity of any kind, but your book compelled me to write you.

Being the second oldest of nine children with an alcoholic father, your story is my story. We ended up with five alcoholics and drug abusers, two overeaters (including me), and two seem fine. I say "seem" fine, because I do not believe that you can come out of that environment unscathed.

My father died in 1972 at age fifty-four, leaving behind unanswered questions too numerous to count. He never sobered up and at the end lived alone. I hadn't seen him for three years before he died.

Today I'm living 2,800 miles away from the rest of my family. I cannot handle family reunions and most of my sibling relationships are fragile, some shattered.

What I've gotten out of my childhood is an inability to trust anyone; constant questioning of my feelings; complete bewilderment over the fact people love me. I spend most days talking myself "up" in hopes of chasing the demons away.

I am in awe of any ACOA who succeeds. It seems to take so much to overcome the fears.

Someday I hope to meet you and share some of my experiences with you. You've overcome; I haven't found the key.

It would be an honor to have you visit our home.
Thank you for an excellent book and, mostly, for hope.

Very sincerely,

Far from Home

Dear Louie,

Thanks for writing the book. I, too, had an erratic, tyrannical father prone to violence. He was not an alcoholic, however. The best my brother and I can come up with was that he was mentally ill. I related to two things in particular in the book. The first was when you presented your story to producers and they said that it didn't sound real; no one could believe it. My brother and I have often said that if anyone knew, they just wouldn't believe some of the things we lived through. He wasn't physically or sexually abusive; he just held the family in a tyrannical kind of mind control with his bizarre behavior. He eventually killed my mother with his behavior.

The other thing that touched me was when you mentioned how you never really knew him. We, too, never really knew my mother. She was so stifled and bewildered by him. He's still alive, but we will never know him either. He now has Alzheimer's disease and is in a locked unit in a nursing home. I visit him often, but he's not sure who I am.

I don't know why I'm telling you all this other than to let you know there are people out there who understand, as you obviously already know.

Yours,
A kindred spirit

Dear Louie

Hi! I am writing to tell you that I think your book is absolutely wonderful!!! I started reading it last night and about halfway through I stopped and called my friend Bob in Long Island to tell him about it. I said, "Bob, this could've been written by you, that is *if* you were a successful comedian from the Midwest, but otherwise, it's you!" His troubled childhood was in Massachusetts and his father was an alcoholic. I should say *is* an alcoholic. And Bob has made a career out of Godiva chocolates and peanut butter and pizza and . . . Bob went to USC to study film and for his senior thesis did a film about his father. His father also had mental problems and was on medication. Let's just say drinking and Thorazine don't mix well. Bob never had friends over for fear of his father's erratic behavior. It's hard enough to get through puberty and be accepted, especially when you are overweight, but it is a horror to have your father lapse into baby talk in front of others. His film is about being a child and watching your father being taken away to the hospital all the time and how it feels not to have a real childhood. Even now he gets upset every time he has to go home for the holidays and face the whole routine over and over. I guess he feels he has to, for his mother's sake.

Anyhow, I woke up early this morning and finished the book and then called my other friend, Joe, and told him about it. Joe is an alcoholic even though he refuses to admit it is a real problem and get help. So the only discussions you can have with him about it are in joke form. His favorite joke is that he can't remember high school at all. Ha ha. So I told him how great your book is and how he should read it and he got all touchy and wanted to know if I was insinuating something about his father. His father, I may add, is dead and never had a drink in his life. I said, "No, you asshole, I'm talking about you." I told him he should read this book before he does something dumb like getting married and reproducing. I can be a real card too, huh?! He says he hasn't had a drink in six months and the thing that finally got him to stop was that when he was driving one night he got hit by an ambulance. It was really the fault of the ambulance and there was so much commotion and all that no one ever stopped to notice that he was totally drunk off his ass and that scared him. In all these years he's never had a DWI or anything. So I told him I'd buy him your book and take him out for an ice cream soda. Joe is one of those disgusting people who could eat twenty ice cream sundaes (with the works) and never gain an ounce. Maybe I'll even fill him in on everything he missed in high school since I was forced to witness it all for him.

So not only did you write an incredible book but now I don't have to wonder what to get them for Christmas.

Anyway, enough about me and all my weird friends. This was supposed to be a fan letter. I used to watch "Hollywood Squares" just to watch you make fun of John Davidson's hair. Now there is a person who probably enjoyed high school gym class!

I think your book is just great and I'm sure everyone else will. I hope you realize how much your fans love you and

support you and need you to get through our crazy lives.
Enjoy the holidays and give your mom a big hug for me.

Best regards and much love,

Honey Lindgren

Dear Louie

I never write. Not to my parents, sister, or brothers. I've sometimes threatened to write to a television station concerning their programming decisions, but I never do. And, when I cried over your description of holding your father when he was near the end, I told myself I must write to this man and let him know what his story has meant to me. Even still, though, I almost didn't. I'm glad I did. It feels good putting things down on paper. Your letters to your dad were the most intimate and powerful collection of self-discovery I've read.

I was in the audience for one of your live shows where you "introduced" your family. Unfortunately the sound was out and the whole thing kind of went to hell but, you know, I felt like I knew what you were trying to say. Please keep saying it. It helps me.

I'm glad you're a Minnesotan. People from other parts of the country associate Minnesota with cold, snow, and Garrison Keillor. And although I'm glad Garrison is a native Minnesotan and I consider him to have captured our "spirit," whatever that means, I want you to exemplify our soul. Happy, witty, wry, but based upon some serious and "unfunny" circumstances.

Boy, that's a cross to bear. I didn't mean to put pressure on you. On second thought, just be you. That will please

us all. If you're ever out our way, the coffeepot is always
on.

Thank you,

A Winneston

Dear Louie

My name is xxxxxxx. I am a friend of A.B. and she introduced me to you last year at the Ohio State Fair. You were nice enough to call me after my cancer was diagnosed. That phone call meant a lot.

I have just finished reading your book. I laughed and I cried. As a codependent and a fellow adult child, I had to write and tell you how much I enjoyed it.

Louie, there is so much pain you have worked through. There were many times I had to stop in between chapters to cry. I felt your pain and your frustration at growing up in a dysfunctional family. I've been working very hard on my own "family of origin" and I was touched by how much healing has gone on in your life for you to write this book.

God has really been working in my life—especially the last year. While I believe I created my cancer, He used it to help me to grow in my faith so that I could face these painful truths of my childhood. I start every day now thanking God for my many blessings—my life and my health are first on the list.

I finished chemotherapy in May and with lots of support from family and friends was able to get through it with a positive attitude and the belief that I am cured. My life continues—better than ever—happy for a second chance.

So, the purpose of this letter is to thank you for caring and to let you know I'm fine—and getting better every day!!

Thanks, too, for having the courage to write your book. It's because of people like you that people like me have the courage to go on with our recovery when sometimes it seems too painful. But as you said, "I'm in too deep to turn back."

God bless,

Getting better all the time

Dear Louie

I enjoy your comedy. I was very impressed with your book. Please write more. This world needs more laughter.

If I could have been one thing it would have been a comedian. It's too late now because I am sixty-three years old, a recovering alcoholic, the mother of four, grandmother of nine, and very grateful to be sober.

Thank you for the story of your life. I laughed, I cried. Thank you. Good luck.

Sincerely,

A Fan

P.S. Surely would like a reply.

Dear Louie

I am writing you as a fellow comedian and the child of an alcoholic father. . . . Your book was sent to me by a friend in the hope that I would learn from it and also ease my pain. You see, my father died three months ago of alcohol-related cirrhosis of the liver and complications brought on by diabetes.

What follows is a copy of my journal entry from that date. I've had to rewrite it because the truck-stop motel this cheap booker put me in doesn't have a copier. So here it is:

It's over. Vinnie died this morning at about 6:45. Vinnie . . . dead. It doesn't even look right on paper. But it is true.

The hospital called the house to let me know. I was surprised at my lack of surprise. There was no wave of shock, no flood of tears. Even at the hospital I couldn't cry.

He was still in his bed when I arrived. There was no sheet covering his face. His mouth was open and with the tube still in his nose one could easily believe he was sleeping.

Except for the deadness. There is an unmistakable sensation one gets around the dead. It is a stillness, a lack of aura or whatever you want to call it but it is undeniably there. I stroked his forehead and talked to him a bit. His skin was still warm but cooling fast. Life leaves very quickly when it's over.

He had a childish quality about him. There was a look of

complete helplessness on his face with a bit of fear mixed in. I could not help wondering, what was it like at the moment of that last heartbeat? What was his very last thought?

It's funny. Over these last couple of years I've played over and over in my mind the scene of our final meeting. There he'd be, on his deathbed fighting for his life with me beside him. I'd be holding his hand and fighting back my tears. And even as he was breathing his last, he would summon up enough breath to look me in the eye and whisper, "I'm sorry." Then he would expire.

But life and death don't run like that movie scene. No, life and death, those two opposing forces that spent seventy years battling one another, conspired on a quiet Sunday morning against me. They took my last chance to square it between us. I've spent this day trying to cry. I can't. Maybe tomorrow or a week from now I will, but right now I can't.

Maybe the relief I felt *was* the proper response. After all, that *is* what I felt. He was finally relieved of the burden of his dying body and I was relieved of the burden of having to watch it die. For once in my life I am also guilt-free. I did what I had to do for him, putting all anger aside.

But will it return? Will I still harbor my anger for him in my heart? I don't know. But my gut tells me probably not. For at thirty-seven years old, I have finally realized that this man was weak in so many areas. He had a disease called alcoholism that ultimately killed him. He died a penniless, broken, unhappy man. I think perhaps life has punished him enough. His memory doesn't need to be soured any more by my vitriol.

And yet, unbeknownst to him, he gave me so many lessons to live by. Without him I would have never known a fear of alcohol and excessive living. Without him I would never have known the true blessings of family and children. Without him I might never have appreciated the grace and beauty of baseball or the precision poetry that is music. Without him I may have never developed my work ethic or self-reliance. These are the things I think I shall remember most about him.

And so Dad, Daddy, Vinnie, or whatever I happened to be calling you at any given age, the time has come when we must part for now. I trust and hope that wherever you are, God has instructed you to watch over your children and grandchildren. I hope that He has imbued you with wisdom and the ability to offer some guidance to those you left behind. But most of all I hope that He has granted you that thing which you so desperately and futilely sought here—a sense of contentment. That is what I wish for you most of all.

I have questioned often in my thirty-seven years whether or not I loved you. God knows that there were times when I wanted to kill you myself. There were times when I hated you so—well you know how it was.

But I remember so well being a child and how just the sight of you made my heart leap. I adored you, Vinnie. And perhaps that was my mistake. You see, I needed you so much that I elevated you to a place in my heart that no one could breach. I made you almost a god in my childish eyes. So is it any wonder that I was so hurt when I learned the truth? Can you blame me for hating you for not living up to my expectations?

Yet here I am, thirty-seven years old, and I find myself

living in a glass house. I have one failed marriage that left a son behind and I am now remarried with another infant daughter. I realize now that things happen in life that we can't always control. So I have learned to forgive but not forget. For forgetting would only cause me to make the same mistakes you did with *my* kids and *my* life.

So in my final conversation with you I would prefer to say that yes, I loved you. Not because you were the perfect father, which you weren't, or because you were the perfect human being, which you certainly weren't. But I loved you because your heart was good. I loved you because you weren't afraid to dream, which was difficult in a world that punishes dreamers, kills their dreams and chains their lives to despair and frustration. But most of all I loved you because you were a fighter. You never gave up. You fought death right to the end. It had to sneak up behind you and take you while you slept. I know that your first reaction had to be, "You gotta be kidding!"

Good-bye.

So there it is, Louie. It's been three months now and I still think about him every day as I'm sure you think of your dad. But now I know that had he not been in my life, I would never be what I am today. I could not make people laugh at themselves. I could not and neither could you.

Thanks,
Rick Scotti

FOR THE BEST IN PAPERBACKS, LOOK FOR THE

In every corner of the world, on every subject under the sun, Penguin represents quality and variety—the very best in publishing today.

For complete information about books available from Penguin—including Puffins, Penguin Classics, and Arkana—and how to order them, write to us at the appropriate address below. Please note that for copyright reasons the selection of books varies from country to country.

In the United Kingdom: Please write to *Dept. JC, Penguin Books Ltd, FREEPOST, West Drayton, Middlesex UB7 0BR.*

If you have any difficulty in obtaining a title, please send your order with the correct money, plus ten percent for postage and packaging, to *P.O. Box No. 11, West Drayton, Middlesex UB7 0BR*

In the United States: Please write to *Consumer Sales, Penguin USA, P.O. Box 999, Dept. 17109, Bergenfield, New Jersey 07621-0120.* VISA and MasterCard holders call 1-800-253-6476 to order all Penguin titles

In Canada: Please write to *Penguin Books Canada Ltd, 10 Alcorn Avenue, Suite 300, Toronto, Ontario M4V 3B2*

In Australia: Please write to *Penguin Books Australia Ltd, P.O. Box 257, Ringwood, Victoria 3134*

In New Zealand: Please write to *Penguin Books (NZ) Ltd, Private Bag 102902, North Shore Mail Centre, Auckland 10*

In India: Please write to *Penguin Books India Pvt Ltd, 706 Eros Apartments, 56 Nehru Place, New Delhi 110 019*

In the Netherlands: Please write to *Penguin Books Netherlands bv, Postbus 3507, NL-1001 AH Amsterdam*

In Germany: Please write to *Penguin Books Deutschland GmbH, Metzlerstrasse 26, 60594 Frankfurt am Main*

In Spain: Please write to *Penguin Books S. A., Bravo Murillo 19, 1° B, 28015 Madrid*

In Italy: Please write to *Penguin Italia s.r.l., Via Felice Casati 20, I-20124 Milano*

In France: Please write to *Penguin France S. A., 17 rue Lejeune, F–31000 Toulouse*

In Japan: Please write to *Penguin Books Japan, Ishikiribashi Building, 2–5–4, Suido, Bunkyo-ku, Tokyo 112*

In Greece: Please write to *Penguin Hellas Ltd, Dimocritou 3, GR–106 71 Athens*

In South Africa: Please write to *Longman Penguin Southern Africa (Pty) Ltd, Private Bag X08, Bertsham 2013*